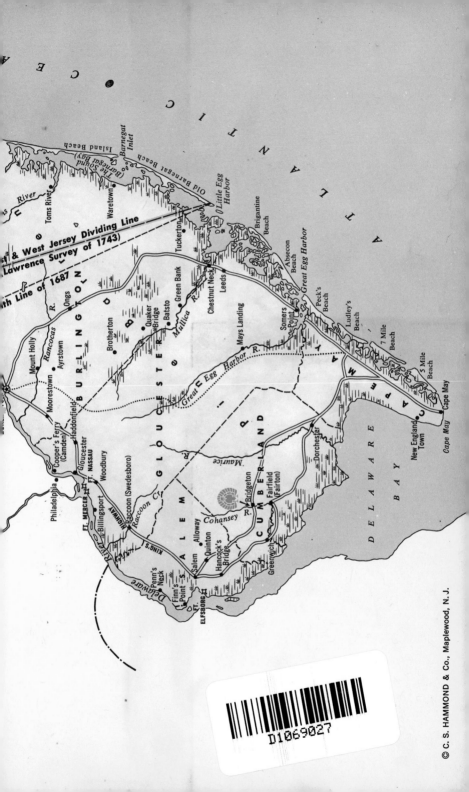

D1069027

The Early Dutch and Swedish Settlers of New Jersey

THE NEW JERSEY HISTORICAL SERIES

Edited by

RICHARD M. HUBER   WHEATON J. LANE

Other books in the series will be announced

Volume 10

The New Jersey Historical Series

The Early Dutch and Swedish Settlers of New Jersey

ADRIAN C. LEIBY

1964

D. VAN NOSTRAND COMPANY, INC.

Princeton, New Jersey

New York, N. Y. • Toronto, Canada • London, England

D. VAN NOSTRAND COMPANY, INC.
120 Alexander St., Princeton, New Jersey (*Principal office*)
24 West 40 Street, New York 18, New York

D. VAN NOSTRAND COMPANY, LTD.
358, Kensington High Street, London, W.14, England

D. VAN NOSTRAND COMPANY (*Canada*), LTD.
25 Hollinger Road, Toronto 16, Canada

PRINTED IN THE UNITED STATES OF AMERICA

To My Wife
Emorie Atkins Leiby

FOREWORD

Many tracks will be left by the New Jersey Tercentenary celebration, but few will be larger than those made by the New Jersey Historical Series. The Series is a monumental publishing project—the product of a remarkable collaborative effort between public and private enterprise.

New Jersey has needed a series of books about itself. The 300th anniversary of the State is a fitting time to publish such a series. It is to the credit of the State's Tercentenary Commission that this series has been created.

In an enterprise of such scope, there must be many contributors. Each of these must give considerably of himself if the enterprise is to succeed. The New Jersey Historical Series, the most ambitious publishing venture ever undertaken about a state, was conceived by a committee of Jerseymen—Julian P. Boyd, Wesley Frank Craven, John T. Cunningham, David S. Davies, and Richard P. McCormick. Not only did these men outline the need for such an historic venture; they also aided in the selection of the editors of the series.

Both jobs were well done. The volumes speak for themselves. The devoted and scholarly services of Richard M. Huber and Wheaton J. Lane, the editors, are a part of every book in the series. The editors have been aided in their work by two fine assistants, Elizabeth Jackson Holland and Bertha DeGraw Miller.

To D. Van Nostrand Company, Inc. my special thanks for recognizing New Jersey's need and for bringing their skills and publishing wisdom to bear upon the printing and distributing of the New Jersey Historical Series.

My final and most heartfelt thanks must go to Adrian C. Leiby, who accepted my invitation to write *The Early Dutch and Swedish Settlers of New Jersey,* doing so at great personal sacrifice and without thought of material gain. We are richer by his scholarship. We welcome this important contribution to an understanding of our State.

RICHARD J. HUGHES
*Governor of the
State of New Jersey*

January, 1964

PREFACE

New Netherland, and not least of it Dutch New Jersey, is greater than the sum of its parts. It would deserve a place in history if it had produced nothing but the Dutchmen of Washington Irving's wonderful imagination: the simple, good-natured fellow of the name of Rip Van Winkle, the bumbling, cheerful, obtuse, self-assured Dutchmen of Knickerbocker's *History of New York,* and the Jersey Dutchmen of Communipaw, who,

. . . like wise men and sound philosophers . . . never look beyond their pipes; nor trouble their heads about any affairs out of their immediate neighborhood; so that they live in profound and enviable ignorance of all of the troubles, anxieties and revolutions of this distracted planet, [and] verily believe that Holland, of which they have heard so much from tradition, is situated somewhere on Long Island. . . .

. . . The Dutch New Jersey of Washington Irving was the wonderful place

whither the primitive manners of our Dutch forefathers have retreated . . . where the dress of the original settlers is handed down inviolate from father to son, the identical broad-brimmed hat, broad-skirted coat and broad-bottomed breeches . . . and several gigantic knee buckles of massy silver . . . that made gallant display in the days of the patriarchs.

His Communipaw was not the Communipaw of reality, certainly not the Communipaw where Captain Guert Tysen and his freebooters from the Spanish Main celebrated their exploits, and the Dutchmen of Knickerbocker's *History* were not the Dutchmen who opened the

Jersey wilderness, but no one need concern himself for a moment about that. The New Netherland that Washington Irving made part of the American heritage will survive long after all of the histories of the Jersey Dutch has been written and forgotten.

Many people helped me to prepare this book. Mr. Donald S. Sinclair, the Director of Special Collections of the Rutgers University Library, has suggested much source material and has been most helpful in reviewing the manuscript. Mr. Fred Van Dyke, of Bergenfield, has spent a great deal of time on the photographs; Mr. Samuel Staeger, of the Cadmus Book Store, in New York City, has helped me to collect relevant material, particularly books relating to the Swedes in New Jersey; and the staff of the Map Division of the Library of Congress have been helpful in their field. I am indebted to Dr. John E. Pomfret and Dr. Wesley Frank Craven for their suggestions, and to Mr. Frederick W. Bogert, Mr. Richard Amerman, and Mr. Lewis Owen. Dr. Simon Hart, the Archivist of the City of Amsterdam, an authority on the early Dutch in America, was kind enough to locate the portraits of Michiel Pauw and Godard Van Reede Van Nederhorst and to search out and translate several Dutch manuscripts relating to New Jersey people in his archives. Mr. Tell G. Dahllöf, of Stockholm, the editor of the Swedish magazine *Industria,* a collector of books and manuscripts about the Swedes in America, reviewed the material about the Swedish settlements and obtained manuscripts and other material for me in Sweden, and Mr. Carl M. Anderson, of Summit, has translated early Swedish material. I am indebted to Mr. Albert T. Klyberg, Jr., of Hackensack, for his suggestions and his help in preparing the manuscript, and even more so to my wife, who has worked from the outset on every aspect of the book. I am most grateful to all of them.

ADRIAN C. LEIBY

Bergenfield, New Jersey
January, 1964

❧ x ☙

TABLE OF CONTENTS

LIST OF ILLUSTRATIONS

I

NEW NETHERLAND

B<small>Y THE TIME</small> of the Revolution, New Jersey was the admiration of all who saw it. An English nobleman found it "verdant and beautiful . . . pleasant, open and well cultivated . . . the garden of America." Others observed that its people were more easy and happy than those of the other colonies. Of all of New Jersey, the Dutch country was the most prosperous; its towns and villages were more impressive; its farms were more fertile and its people more thrifty. The Jersey Dutch dwellings had a peculiar neatness, and ordinary Jersey Dutch people enjoyed an ease and happy competence almost without parallel in their day.

Though they were Calvinists as zealous as any New England Yankee, and almost as frugal in their habits, Jersey Dutchmen avoided the Yankee's austere and puritanical attitudes, and, by 1776, were an outgoing, self-confident people, little resembling the stolid and corpulent Dutchmen of tradition, either in character or appearance: men and women who went cheerfully about their affairs and asked no favors from their English neighbors in any field of endeavor. Most of them spoke and wrote English well enough, though they used plain Dutch in the church and in the family, as a matter of choice.

We need not rely on the reports of admiring colonial travelers for proof of their prosperity. The solid Dutch sandstone farmhouses of the Hackensack and the Raritan valleys, and the valleys of the Passaic, the Saddle River and the Ramapo, and the beautiful Dutch churches which still stand in Neshanic, Hackensack, Paramus, Saddle River, Wyckoff, Bergenfield, and Dumont, all testify to the affluence and character of their Dutch builders. At the outset of the Revolution, the Dutch town of Hackensack was as prosperous as any in the province, the chief river port of northern New Jersey's important iron trade. New Brunswick, at the ferry over the Raritan on the road from New York to Philadelphia, was less favored—"a dismal town, but pleasantly situated," one traveler called it—but it was in the center of an exceedingly rich and beautiful countryside, the banks of the Raritan nearby being covered with gentlemen's houses, at least one of which boasted a Van Dyke and several other valuable Dutch paintings.

A century before, the whole countryside had been a wilderness. A thoughtful traveler in the 1770's could hardly escape the conclusion that the Netherlands had made a far better hand of colonizing America than Great Britain, that in all probability it was America's misfortune that the sturdy Dutch rulers of New York and New Jersey had been displaced by the lackadaisical English. Sensible as that conclusion appeared to be, it was profoundly wrong. Dutch New Jersey owed little if anything to the rule of the Netherlands, if indeed the term rule can be properly applied to fifty years of misrule and neglect. It owed much to the Dutch heritage of its people, whatever their actual origins, and to Dutch religion, customs, and character, but few Dutch virtues had ever been evident in the government of New Netherland by the Dutch West India Company, and some of the best of them had come to the fore only under the rule of the English.

The well-being of the Jersey Dutch may have been traceable neither to their Dutch origins nor to a century of English rule, for by the time of the Revolution Dutch New Jersey showed, perhaps more than any place on the

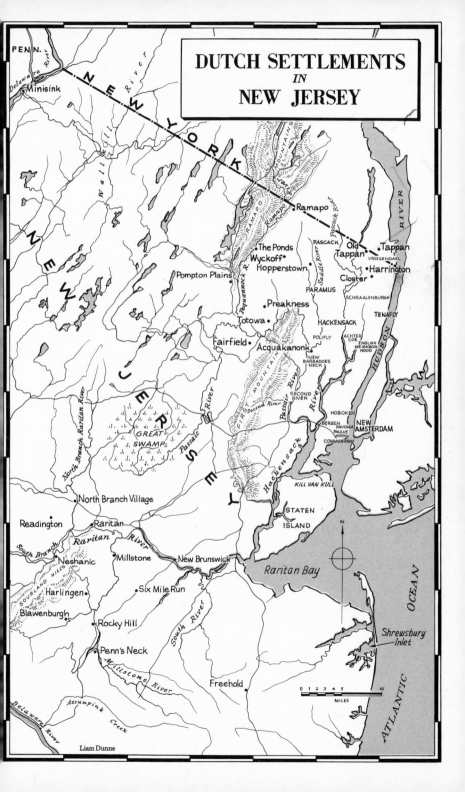

DUTCH SETTLEMENTS
IN
NEW JERSEY

PENN.

Minisink

NEW YORK

NEW JERSEY

Ramapo

The Ponds
Wyckoff•
Hopperstown•
PASCACK
Old
Tappan
Tappan
VRIESENDAEL
Pompton Plains
Closter
Harrington
PARAMUS
SCHRAALENBURGH
Preakness
Totowa•
TENAFLY
HACKENSACK
Fairfield•
Acquakanonk
POLIFLY
ACHTER
COE
ENGLISH
NEIGHBOR-
HOOD
NEW
BARBADOES
NECK
GREAT
SWAMP
SECOND
RIVER
HOBOKEN
BERGEN
PAVONIA
PAULUS
HOOK
COMMUNIPAW
NEW
AMSTERDAM

North Branch Village

Readington
Raritan
Raritan River
Neshanic
Millstone
New Brunswick
Raritan Bay
SOURLAND HILLS
Six Mile Run
Harlingen•
Blawenburgh
Rocky Hill
Penn's Neck
Millstone River

KILL VAN KULL
STATEN
ISLAND

N

Freehold

Shrewsbury
Inlet

ATLANTIC OCEAN

0 1 2 3 4 5   10
MILES

Assunpink Creek
Delaware River

Liam Dunne

continent, the transforming power of the New World, the effect of the thousand and one things that were changing Europeans into Americans in those years. It was not without its European inheritance—at first glance it seemed to show more of the influence of the Old World than New England or Virginia—but its people had put aside the ways of their forefathers and taken on those of America to a greater degree than any people of the western world.

During the preceding century and a half, a few hundred hardy Dutchmen had established an outpost of Dutch civilization on the banks of the Hudson and opened the surrounding wilderness to Dutch settlement, only to see that culture absorbed by a new civilization which, though it retained many Dutch ways, bore little resemblance indeed to eighteenth-century Holland. During the same years, a small outpost of Swedish civilization on the banks of the Delaware had traced the same course.

The Dutch first saw the country that was to be New Jersey in the year 1609, when the ship *Half Moon*, of which Henry Hudson was master and supercargo, sailed into New York Bay under the flag of the Dutch East India Company. Four days after the *Half Moon* anchored, Hudson sent several members of his crew to explore the New Jersey side of the harbor:

There they found a river [the Kill van Kull] to the westward, between two islands. the lands . . . were as pleasant with grass and flowers, and goodly trees, as ever they had seen, and very sweet smells came from them. . . . So they went in about two leagues and saw an open sea [Newark Bay] and returned; as they came back, they were set upon by two canoes, the one having twelve, the other having fourteen men. The night came on, and it began to rain . . . and they had one man slain in the fight . . . an Englishman named John Colman, with an arrow shot into his throat, and two more hurt. It grew so dark that they could not find the ship that night, but labored to and fro on their oars. They had so great a [current] that their grapnell would not hold them.*

Hudson spent a month exploring the river and harbor. On the return voyage he was forced to take leave of the *Half Moon* in England, but the ship and his papers were sent back to the Dutch East India Company. Its directors took no interest in his discoveries and allowed his rough map to be passed on to other merchants, many of whom had been seeking their fortunes abroad for years, and these men quickly saw the possibilities of profit. The short-lived New Netherland Company and some other temporary trading companies were then formed, and their bold and hardy merchant-adventurers opened the Hudson River to the fur trade and laid the way for future settlement.

The first merchant-skipper to visit the Hudson River was Hendrick Christiaensen, who was probably originally a navigator and not a merchant, though he later returned to the Hudson several times to trade, and was murdered by Indians in 1619. Adrian Block, the great navigator for whom Block Island and Block Island Sound are named, was another merchant-adventurer. He once entered his name for a few florins in a lottery, and, as was the custom in that day, added a word for luck: "Everyone seeks his own profit, according to my opinion. . . . If I draw a blank, inform me about it in Amsterdam." He meant nothing by the entry, but it was a fair description of the philosophy of the men who carried the Dutch flag to the New World. They sought their own profit, and if they drew blanks, that was part of the game. Adrian Block, Thijs Volckertsz Mossel, Hans Jorisz Hunthum, Cornelis Rijser, Cornelis Jacobsz May, and Jan deWit were all merchant-navigators with much the same philosophy, and it was not long before they were as well

* J. Franklin Jameson (ed.), *Narratives of New Netherland* (New York, 1909), 18ff.

known to the Indians on the Hudson as they were in Amsterdam, some of them living between voyages in small temporary fortifications along the river. In 1621 the Dutch West India Company was founded, in good degree as a continuation of the efforts of these early traders, and it began the colonization of New Netherland.

The West India Company was chartered to promote trade throughout the western hemisphere by the ruling body of the Netherlands, their High Mightinesses, the States General. Much like the Virginia Company of England in its legal status, it was governed by a board of 19 (the "Nineteen Men"), subject to control by five Chambers situated in different parts of the Dutch Republic, and ultimately to the control of the States General at the Hague. New Netherland was not a very important part of its domains, being looked upon for many years as less promising than its properties in the Caribbean—the islands of Saba, St. Eustatius, St. Martin, and Curaçao—and the colonies of Surinam and Brazil on the South American coast. Indeed, to most of its members, the prospect of privateering on the Spanish Main was far more attractive than colonizing any of its lands.

In March, 1624, the Company sent out Captain Cornelis Jacobsz May, the navigator and explorer for whom Cape May is named, in the *Nieu Nederlandt,* a vessel of 260 tons, with about thirty families aboard, the first Dutch settlers of America. All of them were Walloons, religious refugees who had come to Holland from the French-speaking provinces of the Spanish Netherlands. In the late summer of 1624, May settled 18 of his passengers on Manhattan, 18 others at Fort Orange (Albany), two families and six single men at the Fresh (Connecticut) River, and two families and eight single men, the first settlers of New Jersey, on an island in the Delaware River which is now called Burlington Island, a good distance inland from the sea, probably for protection against Spanish or other hostile warships. The Company was unable to send any substantial number of additional settlers to expand its foothold on the Delaware, but two

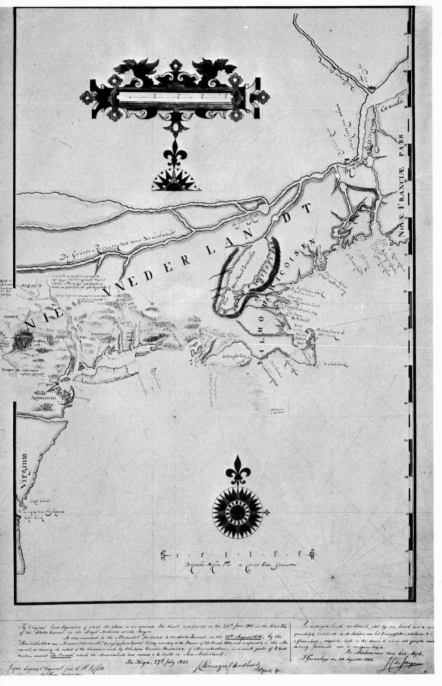

Portion of 1616 map of New Netherland
Courtesy of New York Public Library

years later it established a second small trading post and Indian fort, called Fort Nassau, at the present city of Gloucester. By 1630 a passing Dutch ship reported that the trading house at the Burlington Island settlement stood empty, its settlers having removed to New Amsterdam. Fort Nassau was occupied only intermittently, and never by more than a dozen men. Within a few years the Connecticut River settlements and the settlements on the Delaware were mere trading outposts of New Amsterdam, which itself was hardly in a flourishing condition.

One great difficulty which the West India Company faced was the lack of people to settle its colony, and the reason for the lack of people was the contentment and well-being of the Dutchmen at home. "Colonizing such wild and uncultivated countries demands more inhabitants than we can well supply," the Nineteen Men told the States General, "not so much through the lack of population . . . as from the fact that all who are inclined to do any sort of work procure enough to eat without any trouble and therefore are unwilling to go far from home on an uncertainty."

Another difficulty was the West India Company's conception of New Netherland as a purely business enterprise, a narrow view which its officials narrowed even further, until it embraced little more than the fur trade. Its interest in attracting colonists was small and its efforts to do so were ill-conceived and poorly executed. Its first settlers were hired farmers sent over at its own expense to work on the Company farms, a plan hardly calculated to add much to the numbers of the colony, or, probably, to the character of its people. Later, influenced more by the supposed commercial shrewdness of its businessmen than by broad public considerations, and against the opposition of many of the nobility and public-minded men among the directors, the Company set up a semi-feudal patroon system to induce wealthy men to ship colonists abroad. The scheme excited great hopes of riches in its sponsors, and the prospect of establishing their descendants as lords of manors, but it stirred up

Michiel Pauw, 1590-1640, by P. Moreelse, 1625
Courtesy Iconographisch Bureau, The Hague

controversy among the other directors, and it interested
few who might have been prospective settlers. New Jersey
traces its first permanent settlement to such a patroonship: the Manor of Pavonia. It included most of the

shoreline of modern Jersey City and Hoboken, and seems to have been ably directed and well financed, but in the end, like most of the others, it proved to be a failure.

Michiel Reyniersz Pauw, Heer Van Achttienhoven, registered the patroonship of Pavonia on January 10, 1630. Forty years old at the time, he had been one of the founders of the West India Company in 1621, a director since its foundation, and at one time its ambassador to the French court. He was a nobleman of distinguished Dutch lineage, having inherited the title Lord of Achttienhoven on the death of his father, Reynier Pauw, who had been burgomaster of Amsterdam and ambassador to Denmark, and ultimately one of the States General of the Netherlands. Michiel's brother Adrian was equally prominent, later becoming Grand Pensionary (Prime Minister) of Holland and Zeeland. Michiel Pauw may have been among the directors of the Company who opposed the patroon system, and it was said that he registered his patroonship reluctantly, doing so only because he found that some of his fellow directors (especially the jeweler Killiaen Van Rensselaer, "who was accustomed to refine pearls and diamonds," and other businessmen) were taking the Company's best properties from their partners by the cunning tricks of merchants.

For his own patroonship, Pauw selected one of the most strategic places in New Netherland, the point on the west shore of the Hudson where the Indians had been accustomed for centuries to cross the river to Manhattan and Long Island, at the terminus of all the Indian paths which led from the western mainland to Fort Amsterdam, where his agents could intercept the Indians bringing in furs before they reached the Company's trading post across the river. Moreover, the soil there was exceedingly fertile. A few years later one of Pauw's employees won a wager that he could raise barley on a field seven *morgen* in size (a *morgen* was about two acres) which would grow so tall that he could tie it together over his head anywhere in the field. If Pauw was trying to show the Company that it was a mistake to grant strategic properties to patroons, no better site could have been found. The name of the patroonship, Pavonia, came from *"pavo,"* the Latin for Pauw, meaning "peacock." Its southern part was called Communipa(u)w, the central part Ahasimus, and the northern part Hoboken. The name Paulus Hook, the place where the Indian paths ended at the bank of the river, may be a variant of "Pauw's" Hook.

Pauw proceeded at once to buy the land from the Indians, and set about energetically to develop it, sending over Cornelis Van Vorst as director shortly after he received the grant. Van Vorst brought with him his wife, Vrouwtje, a grown son, Jan, and several other children and grandchildren. Cornelis Van Vorst may well be said to be the first Jerseyman, and New Jersey has every reason to be proud of him. The enemy of all arbitrary restraint, he was one of the fiercely independent men who founded New Netherland, a hard-fighting, hard-drinking, hard-working, contentious man who knew his rights and meant to defend them. He feared neither Indians nor Company officials. Though some writers have disagreed, it is almost certain, since he spoke both French and Dutch fluently, that he came from the village of Vorst, near Antwerp, and not from Voorst, in Gelderland, Holland, and that he was another of the Walloon refugees who made up most of the early settlers of New Netherland, and may well have been one of the many early Walloon fur traders on the Hudson when Pauw chose him to be the director of the manor.

Van Vorst settled himself in Pavonia, back of the salt marsh bordering the Hudson, at Ahasimus (the house was near Henderson and Fifth Streets in modern Jersey City), along the Indian path to the river crossing at Paulus Hook. He traded with the Indians so successfully that when his son Jan went to the Netherlands on the *Eeendracht* in the spring of 1632, he carried with him thousands of beaver skins. As a curiosity, he also took back a number of "sea spiders" (probably native crabs), which, he said, lived by the thousands on the strand in Pavonia.

Pavonia—like New Amsterdam itself—was not fortunate in drawing settlers. In 1633, it was reported that no one but Van Vorst and a few workmen were there, and that Van Vorst was acting more as an Indian trader than as a plantation manager. He was, however, building two houses, one at Communipaw, later occupied by Jan Evertsen Bout, and the other at Ahasimus, for himself.

He was constantly at odds with the Company officials. He once sheltered David Pietersz DeVries at Pavonia when that celebrated Dutch navigator ran afoul of the authorities and left Manhattan a few steps ahead of the Governor's muskets; he would not let the Company's ordinances against Indian trading be posted in Pavonia; and he was always in trouble with the authorities about his own trading.

One of Van Vorst's encounters with a Company official ended in the death of the official. Eight or ten days after Easter, in April, 1634, he traveled upriver to Fort Orange and fell in with an old acquaintance from Antwerp, the Vice-Commander of the colony, Hans Jorisz Hunthum. Having made merry together, an eyewitness said, they crossed the river to see the new house that was being built for Van Rensselaer, and there, after a few more drinks, they began a violent argument in French, during which Van Vorst said that some who had a seat on the council were rogues. Hunthum asked him three times whether he claimed that the members of the council were rogues. Van Vorst said: yes, a part of the council have dealt with me as rogues. Hunthum then jumped up and struck Van Vorst, and Van Vorst, with the blood running from his nose, drew his sword and ran Hunthum through the breast.

Hunthum died instantly. Some colonists said that there was more to the affair than a drinking brawl, that Van Vorst had long before conceived a hatred for Hunthum for posting edicts against Indian trading and had sworn that he would kill him if it took a year.

Few of the settlers blamed Van Vorst in the Hunthum affair. Hunthum was one of the oldest New

Netherland hands and one of the most quarrelsome. The son of an Antwerp fur trader, he had been on the Hudson on board the sloop *Jonge Tobias* as early as 1613, in the days when fur trading consisted more in fighting Dutchmen than in bartering with the natives. Long before New Netherland was founded, Hunthum had made enemies of the merchant-skipper Adrian Block and other traders, and had also made some enemies among the Indians, including the chief sachem of the *Maquaas*, who openly called Hunthum a scoundrel, refusing to trade with him and threatening to kill him if the Indians ever caught him alone in the woods.

After Hunthum's death Van Vorst returned to Pavonia, secure in the knowledge that he had faced and conquered another enemy. A few months later, on August 14, 1634, Governor Wouter Van Twiller reported to the Company that Van Vorst had no respect for authority and still did a great deal of mischief in the Manor of Pavonia, blaming the trouble on the disputes between the patroons and the Company. For Van Vorst's part, he went on about his business, and on September 8, 1634, bought a two-thirds interest in a sloop with a view to expanding his trading activities. In the same year, Michiel Pauw, probably concluding that Van Vorst would be punished for killing Hunthum, sent over Jan Evertsen Bout to take charge of Pavonia. Pauw's patroonship ended shortly thereafter.

During the last few years the opposition to the patroonships had been steadily gaining the upper hand in Holland. Pauw and the other patroons, who had obligated themselves to settle fifty persons on their lands within four years, were accused of defaulting under their agreements, and the Nineteen Men were authorized to buy out their rights. After months of discussion Pauw sold Pavonia for twenty-six thousand florins. The sale probably left him little if any profit in his venture. The patroonships had never been very successful. Only ten were established, of which several (including one on the Jersey side of the Delaware) were never occupied. Swanendael, on the other side of the Delaware, at modern Lewes, was destroyed by Indians in 1630; Rensselaerswyck was the only patroonship that ultimately survived.

Van Vorst continued to occupy the principal bouwerie at Ahasimus after the sale of Pavonia, as a tenant of the Company, and seems to have been on somewhat better terms with the Company officials thereafter. Toward the end of June, 1636, he received a cargo of good Bordeaux wines from New England, and word of their arrival quickly reached his acquaintances on Manhattan Island. It was not long before Governor Van Twiller, Domine Everardus Bogardus, and Captain David DeVries found business across the river. DeVries explained that it was Van Twiller who was fond of tasting good wines, so we may assume that Bogardus and DeVries went along to enjoy the country air, or perhaps to add to their catalog of complaints against Van Twiller, since they were his avowed enemies. As sometimes happens in such cases, there were some words between Van Vorst and Van Twiller and the minister. Van Vorst, who did not want to see his friends part in an angry way, joined them in another bumper or two, so that, as DeVries said, they afterwards parted good friends, but Van Vorst, unsteadied by his efforts at reconciliation, and wishing to give his guests a parting salute, failed to prime and load with his usual skill, with the result that when he "fired a pederero which stood on a palisade before his house . . . a spark flew upon his house, which was thatched with rushes, and in half an hour it was entirely destroyed." It was a Company house, and Van Twiller ordered it rebuilt, but Van Vorst and his family were without shelter for some time thereafter. He died in the summer of 1638. By the time of his death, he had firmly established the first permanent settlement in New Jersey.

Fourteen years had passed since the Dutch West India Company first put its colonists down in America. New Amsterdam, its principal settlement, had prospered somewhat. It held a few hundred people, mostly engaged in small trade, and boasted a counting house, two sawmills, and several substantial houses, including a brick mansion that Van Twiller had built for himself when he was governor. Elsewhere, little progress had been made. The patroon system had been tried and failed, and no one had any other plan that would bring to America the thousands of people who would be needed if New Netherland was ever to rival New England and Virginia. Like every unsuccessful venture, everyone involved had his own reasons for the poor state of the colony, none of them reflecting any credit on the Dutch West India Company, and the Company, for its part, saw little to praise in the people it had sent to settle New Netherland. Four governors in turn had failed to improve matters.

The first governor, Cornelis Jacobsz May, served only briefly. He was followed in 1625 by Willem Verhulst, who was recalled to Holland in disgrace. The next governor was Peter Minuit, a French Huguenot born in Wesel, Germany, best known for buying Manhattan Island from the Indians for 60 guilders—$24—shortly after his arrival on May 4, 1629. Minuit, too, was ordered back to Holland and left the employ of the West India Company immediately thereafter. Wouter Van Twiller, who became governor in the spring of 1633, had never risen above the rank of clerk in the Company's Amsterdam warehouse, but he was a nephew of Killiaen Van Rensselaer, and, as a Dutchman said of another such promotion, had probably been stewed into a governor by keeping the pot closely covered, for he would not have survived any inquiry into his qualifications. Hendrick Hendrickse (Kip), the tailor, described the colonist's feeling about Van Twiller very well when he said that "the *kivit* . . . ought to be packed off to Holland in the *Peacock,* with a letter of recommendation to Master Gerrit and a pound flemish, so that he may give him a nobleman's death." Master Gerrit was the public executioner.

In the spring of 1638, Willem Kieft landed in New

"Manatus . . ." Manuscript map of Manhattan and nearby New Jersey, attributed to J. Vingboons, 1639

Courtesy Library of Congress

Amsterdam at the floating dock near the foot of the present Broad Street and became the fifth governor of New Netherland. His masterful air and suspicious looks made it clear to many in the welcoming crowd that he was no improvement on Wouter Van Twiller. Though their fears were soon proved correct, Willem Kieft's administration saw a considerable expansion of the colony, including some settlement on the west shore of the Hudson. When Kieft arrived, there were only thirty or forty plantations and boweries in all of New Netherland, of which one bouwerie and four plantations were in modern New Jersey. (A bouwerie was a place where the farmer and his family resided; if he resided elsewhere the place was called a plantation.) One plantation was at Jan de Lacher's Hook (Mill Creek Point), one at Paulus Hook, one at Ahasimus immediately to the west of Paulus Hook, and one at Hoboken. The single bouwerie was the Van Vorst place at Ahasimus. Probably no more than a dozen settlers lived west of the river at the time, but the picture was soon to change, for Kieft had brought with him instructions to open the fur trade to the people. The effect was electric. The settlers, feeling that the time had come to make their fortunes, quickly spread themselves far and wide, and many new colonists joined them, including some from Virginia and New England, so that, as one man said, within a few years, in place of seven boweries, thirty were planted and a hundred more were expected.

Settlements were begun at modern Hoboken, Ridgefield Park, and Old Tappan almost at once. On January 1, 1641, Aert Teunissen (Van Putten) leased "a certain bouwerie named *Hoboquin,* situate in Pavonia on the west side of the North River," for the term of ten years and proceeded to fence the land, clear the fields, and build a new house. He "brought thither eight and twenty head of large cattle, besides various more stock, swine, goats, etc. and sheep, together with many of his own fruit trees," and settled himself there with his wife, children, and servants.

Godard Van Reede Van Nederhorst, 1588-1648, by Gerard Ter Borsch.
Courtesy Iconographisch Bureau, The Hague

A settlement called Achter Col was begun at the junction of the Hackensack and the Overpeck, at the place later known as Old Hackensack (modern Ridgefield Park), within a few hundred paces of a large village of Hackensack Indians. Achter Col, or Achter t'Col, means "back of the pass." It was a name variously used to describe Newark Bay, the Hackensack River itself, the country along the Hackensack River, and, in the years of the Dutch reoccupation of New Jersey, all of northern New Jersey. It survives in the corruption Arthur Kill. (The name Kill van Kull, "river of the pass," suggests that the pass referred to was the channel between modern Bayonne and Staten Island.) The Achter Col settlement was part of a large grant of land extending from Hoboken as far north as Tappan which had recently been made to Myndert Myndertsen (Van Keren) and his partner, Godard Van Reede, Heer Van Nederhorst. Van Nederhorst, like Michiel Pauw, was a nobleman of a prominent Dutch family, who was not only Lord of Nederhorst, but of Kortenhoef, Hosterweerd, Vreeland, and Overmeer as well. He had been active in canal and reclamation projects near his native Utrecht, and he and his family were well known and well connected in diplomatic circles in the Netherlands and abroad. Van Nederhorst had also recently acquired a half-interest in Cornelis Melyn's Staten Island colony. The agent of Van Nederhorst and Myndertsen in America was Johannes Winckelman, who came to Staten Island in the winter of 1641 and first settled his people and cattle there. He left shortly and commenced the new colony at Achter Col, evidently without consulting Melyn, because Melyn took the matter to court, where Winckelman's defense was that he had come out as a servant of Myndertsen and was acting under Myndertsen's orders when he moved the colony.

The third settlement, called Vriesendael, was begun by Captain David Pietersz DeVries north of the Achter Col colony, on the Indian maize land back of the Hudson near the Tappen Zee. DeVries described his house at Vriesendael as one made with embrasures through which his farmers could defend themselves against Indian attack. Vriesendael also boasted a second farmhouse, a barn, tobacco house, and small brewery, altogether a property which would have been most impressive in Old Tappan a century later.

Though Achter Col and Vriesendael and other similar settlements gave an air of prosperity to New Netherland, and might have ultimately developed into settled communities, they added little to the strength of the colony. Situated as they were almost a day's journey from New

Amsterdam, they were for the moment little more than trading posts designed to intercept Indians on their way to the Company's posts, and as Company officials pointed out, merely exposed the settlers to the danger of Indian attacks, particularly since (if the Company reports were to be believed) they had been placed there against the will of the Indians themselves. Whether or not the Indians opposed them, the white man's recklessness in settling near Indians to have first call on their beaver pelts was most imprudent, and was one of a chain of events that almost destroyed New Netherland. The decision to open the Indian trade to everyone, though hailed by the people, was a mistake. What New Netherland needed was farmers, not more fur traders.

The Indians became more and more aggressive as the Dutch sought their favor in trade. (One official complained that the traders, not being satisfied with merely taking the Indians into their houses in the customary way, were "admitting them to the table, laying napkins before them, presenting wine to them and more of that kind of thing.") Thinly populated as it was, the colony had always been in danger of Indian attack. Swanendael had been wholly destroyed by Indians in 1630, and its people murdered. In 1641, many of the settlers in a colony that Captain David DeVries had established on Staten Island were murdered by Raritan Indians. DeVries claimed that the trouble had been stirred up by some of the Company's soldiers, and he may have been right in the particular case, but many an isolated settler had been murdered for nothing more than an imagined Dutch insult.

One murder occurred almost within sight of the fort at New Amsterdam, on the Company's Bouwerie Number Five. An Indian came to Claes Swits Rademacher and offered to trade beavers with him for duffles cloth. When Rademacher stooped down to take the goods out of a locked chest, the Indian seized an ax standing behind him and struck him dead. The murderer claimed that years before a Dutchman had taken beavers from his uncle and killed him and that when he was a small boy he had resolved to revenge the deed upon the Dutch when he grew up.

Another settler was murdered at Achter Col, a murder which Captain DeVries almost witnessed. Achter Col was only a short hour's journey below Vriesendael. On one of his visits to the settlement to see how it was progressing, DeVries met a drunken Indian, five or six hundred paces from the village. The Indian came up to him and stroked his arms, which was a gesture of friendship among them, and said that DeVries was a good chief, that when they came to his house he let them have milk and everything for nothing, but that he had just come from Achter Col, where they had sold him brandy which was half water, that he could scoop up the water himself from the river and had no need of buying it. He also said they had stolen his beaver coat. He said he was going home to get his bow and arrows to shoot some one of the villainous Dutchmen, who had stolen his goods. DeVries tried to pacify the Indian, telling him that he must not kill anyone, then went on to the main house and told the people there that they must stop mistreating the savages, as they were a very revengeful people, resembling the Italians in that particular. After a while he returned to Vriesendael, shooting a thirty-pound wild turkey on the way. It was not long before some chiefs came from Hackensack and from Reckawanck, which was close by, and told DeVries that one of their Indians who was drunk had shot and killed a Dutchman while he was thatching the roof of his barn at Achter Col. They asked what they should do, since they dared not go to the fort, and offered one or two hundred fathom of *zeewan* (wampum: Indian shell currency) to the widow if that would settle the matter. DeVries took them to Governor Kieft, who said that he wanted the murderer brought to him. The chiefs said that they could not bring him, because he had run away a two days' journey, but if Kieft would listen to them, they would pay for the man's death with *zeewan*. They laid the blame upon Dutchmen who sold

David Pietersz De Vries, 1594-1655

brandy or wine to the young Indians, making them crazy, as they were unaccustomed to drink. They had, they said, frequently seen even Dutchmen, who were used to strong drink, intoxicated and fighting with knives. They told Kieft that the Dutchmen ought to stop selling liquor to the Indians if they wanted to prevent such accidents in the future. On the way home, the savages told DeVries that they could not deliver the murderer as he was a Sackamaker's son, that is, a chief's son. The man who was killed was Garret Jansen Van Vorst, of Ahasimus, son of Jan Van Vorst and a grandson of Cornelis Van Vorst. He left a wife and a young son.

In the 1640's there were no settlements west of the Hudson beyond Achter Col and Vriesendael until one reached the banks of the Delaware on the south, or Esopus Creek (Kingston) on the north. This then—so far as the country which was to be called New Jersey was concerned—was the Dutch West India Company's domain a year or two after Kieft's arrival: one bouwerie of a few cultivated acres, several plantations with less, and the beginnings of two or three Indian trading posts. Small as the domain was, it was soon to be diminished.

II

NEW SWEDEN

In 1638, a new difficulty was thrown in the way of the Dutch West India Company by a group of Dutchmen acting under a Swedish charter, who established a competing colony on the South River (the Delaware). The group in fact included some of the old partners of the West India Company.

The seventeenth century was the age of great commercial trading companies. In these, as in other matters of business, the Dutch were far and away the leaders of the world. The Danish East India Company, for example, was only a Dutch company flying a flag of convenience, as were the Swedish South Sea and Africa Companies. In the first half of the seventeenth century, one historian has said, the Dutch established an almost complete control over the economic life of Sweden. The man who had been chiefly responsible for founding the Dutch West India Company was Willem Usselinx, a Walloon who combined great energy at business with an unrelenting hatred for Spain. When he saw that the Dutch West India Company was not likely to produce any great results, he left the Netherlands to go to Danzig to associate himself with a Dutch mercantile house there. On the way, he stopped at Gothenburg, Sweden, and in October, 1624, he was granted an audience with King Gustavus Adolphus, then perhaps the principal military figure of Europe. The King was much impressed by the

commercial rhapsodies of Usselinx, just as the businessmen of the Netherlands had been, and Usselinx soon had
a charter to establish a Swedish general trading company
"for Asia, Africa, America, and Magellenica." Several
charters followed, as Usselinx moved back and forth between Sweden, Holland, and Germany with his grandiose
plans. (Like many other promoters, he found that it was
easier to get stock subscriptions than to collect them and
easier to start companies than to make them prosper.)
One of the enterprises inspired by Usselinx's activities
was the New Sweden Company, which, though no more
prosperous than the rest, was destined to cause the Dutch
West India Company a great deal of trouble.

In its beginnings, at least, Dutchmen owned as much
of the New Sweden Company as did Swedes. Its principal
promoter was Samuel Blommaert, a prominent businessman of Amsterdam who had been one of the most active
sponsors of the Swanendael settlement of the Dutch West
India Company on the South River, which had ended in
an Indian massacre. Peter Spiring, a Dutch businessman
in Sweden, was another of the promoters. The two principal Swedish investors were Klas Larson Fleming, a
Finn, the head of the Swedish naval office, and Axel
Oxenstierna, Gustavus Adolphus' prime minister.

In the fall of 1635, it was decided to send Peter
Minuit—who had left the employ of the West India
Company with hard feelings on both sides—to found a
Swedish colony on the South River; at the very place, in
fact, where Blommaert and Minuit had recently failed to
establish the Swanendael colony under Dutch auspices.
With Minuit's help and Swedish protection, why could
not a new Dutch-Swedish company take over the South
River, a place the West India Company had failed to
colonize and could not protect? Minuit was able to supply part of the capital himself and other Dutch capitalists
could readily be found to join so promising a venture.
Half of the capital required was to be raised in Holland,
the other half in Sweden. Minuit was to lead the expedition and manage the colonial affairs; Blommaert was to

direct the business of the Company in Holland. He was to buy goods for the expedition, make other necessary preparations, and draft the proposals for privileges, to be laid before the Swedish Government. The Swedish Government was expected to furnish soldiers for the new colony and protection for the Company's ships. Finally, in August, 1637, a charter was issued, and Minuit carried it to Amsterdam, where Blommaert had been busy buying cloth and other merchandise for the Indian trade, and engaging sailors, who were difficult to hire in Sweden. The sailors and officers, together with a large part of the cargo, were sent to Sweden in the summer. Two ships were furnished by the Swedish government: the *Kalmar Nyckel* (the *Key of Kalmar*) and the *Fogel Grip* (the legendary Griffin: half-lion, half-eagle), both under Dutch masters. In early November the two little vessels put out from Gothenburg with the first Swedish-American emigrants to the New World. They were soon separated by fearful winter storms. It took the *Kalmar Nyckel* a month's cruising about to arrive at Texel in Holland, and then without a prow or mainmast. The smaller *Fogel Grip* arrived a week later, also badly damaged.

Few Dutchmen at Texel seemed concerned about the probable destination of the two ships. In fact, Killiaen Van Rensselaer, an old friend of Peter Minuit and a former partner of Blommaert, took the opportunity to send six colonists to Rensselaerswyck on them. One of the six was the progenitor of the Jersey Dutch Blauvelt family, seventeen-year-old Gerrit Hendricksen, of Deventer. On December 31, 1637, after many delays, the two ships put out from Texel for America.

They reached the Delaware River in the middle of March, 1638. The Dutch claimed that Minuit told the Netherlanders at Fort Nassau, the Dutch post on the river, that he was on a voyage to the West Indies, and that, passing by there, he wished to arrange some matters and to furnish the ship with water and wood and would then leave. "Some time afterwards," they went on,

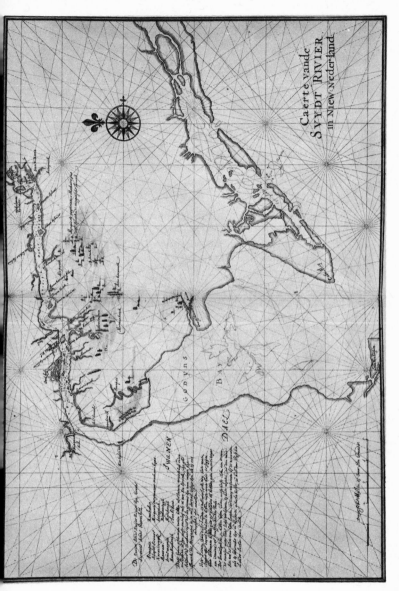

"Suydt Rivier . . . in Niew Nederland" Manuscript map of
Delaware River and Bay, attributed to J. Vingboons, 1639
Courtesy Library of Congress

some of our people going again found the Swedes still there, but then they had already made a small garden for raising salads, pot herbs and the like. They wondered at this and inquired of the Swedes what it meant and whether they intended to stay there. They excused themselves by various reasons and subterfuges. . . . The third time it became apparent, from their building a fort, what their intentions were. . . . The Swedes, with intolerable insolence, have thrown down the [Dutch] arms . . . and since they are suffered to remain so, this is looked upon by them and particularly by their government as a Roman achievement. True, we have made several protests . . . but they have had as much effect as the flying of a crow overhead. . . .*

Minuit, having put down his first settlers, left New Sweden in the *Kalmar Nyckel* a few months after his arrival. While his ship was anchored at St. Christopher in the West Indies, a hurricane struck the port. Minuit was not aboard the *Kalmar Nyckel* at the time, but was visiting the master of the *Vliegende Hert* (Flying Stag), a Dutch merchantman. Both ships put out to sea to ride out the storm. The *Flying Stag* was never seen again, and Minuit went down with the ship. His death was a great blow to Sweden's plans in America.

Minuit's successor was Peter Hollander Ridder, a Dutchman who had been in the Swedish service for years. Great efforts were made to gather colonists, particularly blacksmiths, shoemakers, brickmakers, carpenters, and the like, but it was difficult to find people in Sweden willing to migrate on their own accord, and the Swedish government was forced, in order to enlarge the small foothold which it had established on the South River, to impress soldiers who had deserted and others who had committed crimes "such that people did not shun their company." Ridder arrived in America in April, 1640, and began energetically to buy up Indian lands, including much of the New Jersey shore of the Delaware tide-

* J. Franklin Jameson (ed.), *Narratives of New Netherland* (New York, 1909), 315.

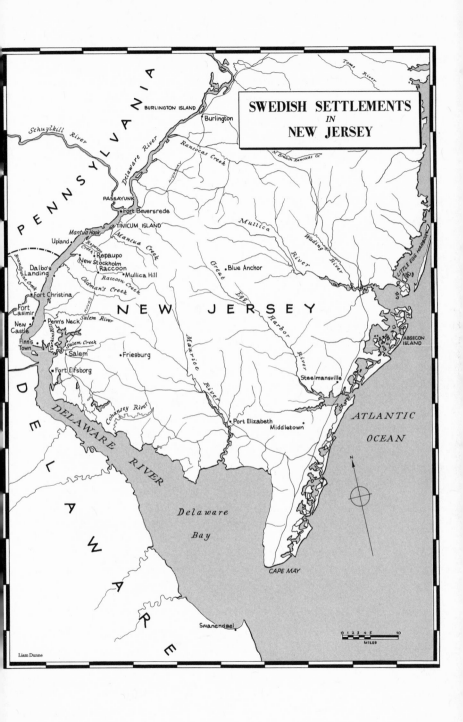

SWEDISH SETTLEMENTS
IN
NEW JERSEY

BURLINGTON ISLAND

Burlington

PENNSYLVANIA

Schuylkill River

Delaware River

Rancocas Creek

N. Branch Rancocas Cr.

Toms River

HIGHWAY

PASSAYUNK

Fort Beversrede

Mullica River

TINICUM ISLAND

Mantua Hook

Mantua Creek

Upland

Repaupo Creek

Repaupo

New Stockholm

Raccoon

Mullica Hill

Raccoon Creek

Oldman's Creek

Great Egg Harbor River

Wading River

LITTLE EGG HARBOR BAY

Blue Anchor

Dalbo's Landing

Brandywine Creek

Fort Christina

NEW JERSEY

ABSECON ISLAND

Fort Casimir

Penn's Neck

Salem River

New Castle

Stockholm River

Salem Creek

Finn's Town

Salem

Friesburg

Maurice River

Staelmansville

Fort Elfsborg

Cohansey River

Fort Elizabeth

Middletown

ATLANTIC

OCEAN

DELAWARE RIVER

DELAWARE

Delaware Bay

N

CAPE MAY

Swanendael

Liam Dunne

0 1 2 3 4 5   10
MILES

water, though he was in no position to settle so large a territory.

The Swedes and the Dutch lost little love on each other. The two Dutch officers of the *Kalmar Nyckel,* which brought Ridder to America, a Swede complained, stayed in the cabin during the whole voyage, smoking and drinking, *"met brandewign en toeback melcander,"* and scolding the Swedes. The more they drank and the more they reflected on their Swedish passengers, the more incensed they became at the Lutheran religion, and at poor Reverend Reorus Torkillus, its representative aboard the ship, who had probably been doing nothing but trying to swallow a little solid food and live through the crossing. The Swedes, for their part, were busy laying plans to send all of the Dutchmen in the colony back home as soon as they could get along without them.

In February, 1641, the Swedish government bought out the Dutch shares in the New Sweden Company, and thereafter it was operated entirely in the interests of Sweden, although Dutchmen continued to be active in its affairs. With the New Sweden Company virtually under control of the government, new efforts were made to increase the population. The usual roundup of emigrants was undertaken, and the haul again consisted principally of poachers, deserters from the army, debtors, and others who were in one legal difficulty or another. Many of them were Finns, who were in trouble with the authorities because of the new edict against clearing land by burning it over, some being given the choice of hanging or going to America. Two were said to be married men who had committed adultery three times, one of whom had in addition shot some elks on Åland. Among the passengers on one ship was Herr Christoffer, a young minister, who "goes along on the recommendation of the Royal Admiral, who also gave him 100 *dalers* copper money . . . from his own means. Otherwise he had demanded nothing besides his board, because he only wishes to gain some experience or try his luck." There were several other adventurous souls of the same turn of mind. Another passenger was Måns Kling, who had come home from America to get his wife and young child. Governor Ridder was not impressed by his colonists, complaining that it would be impossible to find more stupid people in all Sweden and that not one of them could build a common peasant's house or saw a board. One cargo of the Company's emigrants consisted almost entirely of Dutchmen from Utrecht, sponsored by Godard Van Reede, Heer Van Nederhorst, who was also sponsoring a Dutch colony on the Hackensack River in New Netherland at the same time. Within a few years the Utrecht Dutchmen all drifted northward to New Netherland.

Ridder made little progress as governor, and the authorities at home soon relieved him of his post and appointed Johan Printz in his place. Printz ruled New Sweden from 1643 to 1653. The son of a clergyman, he had prepared for a learned vocation, studying Latin, philosophy, and theology in both Sweden and Germany. He nevertheless entered military service, where he had a distinguished if somewhat unlucky career under several flags, his latest service being as lieutenant colonel of the Vastgotha (West Gotha) Cavalry Regiment. He had been knighted by the Swedish government just before his appointment to the American post. The Indians called him "big belly." DeVries said that he weighed over four hundred pounds. Despite his great weight, his friends claimed that he was a man of action, severe but not cruel, strict but not arbitrary, and always a zealous defender of the interests of Sweden. His critics called him furious and passionate, cursing and swearing upon every occasion, arrogant, choleric, dictatorial, extravagant in his tastes and love of luxury, and some criticized the small fortune he made in America. There was evidence to support both his friends and his enemies.

Johan Printz was an effective governor, and whatever successes New Sweden enjoyed in its short life it owed largely to him. As soon as he arrived in America and made an inspection tour of the colony, he began to build

Johann Printz, 1592-1663. Copy of contemporary painting at
Bottnaryd, Sweden

Courtesy American Swedish Historical Museum

a fort on the eastern banks of the Delaware in what is
now New Jersey. He chose a high point several miles
below the mouth of Varkins Kill (Salem Creek) and there
built Fort Elfsborg, on a natural promontory command-

ing the river. The fort has become more famous as *Myggenborg,* or "Mosquito Castle," than for anything else, and it has long since been inundated by a change in the course of the river, but in its day it was an important military post. When the fort was completed, with Lieutenant Sven Skute in command, a settlement of about a hundred Englishmen from the New Haven colony who had been living in the vicinity, harassed by sickness, threatened by the home authorities in London, and on the point of breaking up, came under the protection of Governor Printz and the Swedes, as Swedish citizens. Swedish accounts said they came willingly; others said Printz dragooned them.

III

THE 1643 INDIAN WAR

By the early 1640's, all of New Netherland was incensed by the Indian outrages and demanded that Governor Kieft do something to stop them. He sent some soldiers to try to punish the Indians who had killed Claes Rademacher on the Company's Bouwerie Number Five, but they lost their way in the darkness and arrived too late in the day to effect any surprise. They returned without doing anything, and a few days later another expedition also miscarried. People began to reproach Governor Kieft with "keeping himself protected in a good fort, out of which he had not slept a single night in all the years he had been there," while they faced the Indians. Kieft finally called the people together to choose twelve men (the "Twelve Men") to share the responsibility for dealing with the problem. The Twelve Men, who saw as clearly as Kieft that great risk was involved in an Indian war, were reluctant to advise an open attack. They felt that time and opportunity must be taken, that it would not be expedient to carry on a war with the savages until, like the English, they had enough people to make towns and villages. Captain David DeVries, the patroon of Vriesendael, told Kieft that he was certain that the West India Company disapproved any war against the savages, for in the year 1630, when his people on the South River had been murdered through some trifling acts of the commander, it was proposed to the Company to make war upon the savages, but the Com-

pany would not permit it. Some people, quick to blame
the Governor for any trouble, suspected him of conniving
with the Indians. While he was seeking in vain for a
solution, the Mahiken Indians started a war against the
Indians of the Westchester tribe that had killed Rademacher, killing 70 of them and taking many women and
children away to captivity. The survivors fled to New
Amsterdam, where they were received into the houses
and fed by the director for 14 days. Shortly after, seized
with another panic, they fled with the Hackensacks, fully
a thousand strong, first to the vicinity of the fort and
then over the river to Pavonia.

Cornelis Van Tienhoven, the Company's secretary, and
Corporal Hans Steen were sent over to Pavonia to scout
the Indian camp. which lay near Jan Evertsen Bout's
bouwerie, and other scouts were sent to Corlear's bouwerie, on Manhattan Island, to reconnoitre an Indian
camp there. (Corporal Steen may have been happy to
have the opportunity. Not long before, he had been
prosecuted for fornication, and sentenced to three hours
on the wooden horse and reduced to the ranks for 14 days
as punishment.) The most detailed account of the events
of the next few days was written by David DeVries, whose
hatred for Kieft and Van Tienhoven probably colored
it considerably. DeVries said that he had come down to
New Amsterdam from Tappan to get some soldiers to
help him, as he put it, make himself master in his own
house by removing some Indians who would not get out.
He was amazed to find that the Governor was about to
attack the Indians at Pavonia and Corlear's Hook, using
the excuse that Maryn Adriansen, Jacob Planck, and
Jan Damen had petitioned him to do so while he was
dining with them at Damen's house. Adriansen, Damen,
and Planck were three of the Twelve Men, and Kieft
insisted that they could act for all. Planck and Adriansen,
who were sons-in-law of Damen, had plantations at
Paulus Hook and Hoboken, but probably did not live on
the Jersey side of the river at the time. DeVries pleaded
that an attack on the Indians would "also murder our

own nation, for there are none of the settlers in the open country who are aware of it," but Kieft's only reply was to tell him to go to the large hall which he had lately added to his house. There, DeVries said, stood all of Kieft's soldiers ready to cross the river to Pavonia and commit the murder. DeVries remained at the Governor's house that night, February 25, 1643, sitting up by the kitchen fire. "About midnight I heard a great shrieking and went to the ramparts of the fort and looked over to Pavonia, saw nothing but firing and heard the shrieks of the savages murdered in their sleep."

The soldiers massacred 80 Indians and took about forty prisoners at Pavonia. Forty more were massacred in their sleep at Corlear's bouwerie by an expedition under Maryn Adriansen. Most of the colonists were incensed. "Did the Duke of Alba in the Netherlands," they asked, "ever do anything more cruel? This is indeed a disgrace to our nation."

If there were any Dutchmen who were not appalled by the cynicism and cruelty of the massacres, they were soon appalled by the consequences. The Hackensack Indians joined thousands of Indians of other tribes to revenge themselves upon the Dutch and drive them out of the country. They killed all the men they could surprise on the farmlands, they burned all the houses and farm buildings and destroyed everything that came within their reach. The people told the States General some months later:

We poor inhabitants of New Netherland were here in the spring pursued by those wild heathens and barbarous savages with fire and sword; daily in our houses and fields they cruelly murdered men and women with hatchets and tomahawks, struck little children dead in their parents' arms or before their doors; or carried them away into bondage; the houses and grain barracks are burnt with the produce; cattle of all descriptions are slain and destroyed and such as remain must perish, with the approach of winter, for the want of fodder. Almost every place is abandoned. We, wretched people, must skulk, with wives and little ones that still survive, in poverty together in and around the fort at Manhattan, where we are not safe even for an hour, whilst the Indians daily threaten to overwhelm us. . . . The enemy meets with scarcely any resistance. The garrison consists of but fifty or sixty soldiers unprovided with ammunition. Fort Amsterdam, utterly defenseless, stands open to the enemy night and day. . . . The fort is . . . entirely out of order and resembles (with deference) rather a mole hill than a fort against an enemy.*

Almost all of the country west of the Hudson was laid waste by the first Indian attacks. Aert Teunissen's family at Hoboken was nearly wiped out. He himself was attacked and killed while on his sloop trading in the Shrewsbury Inlet, and his children and servants were murdered at home. Only his wife escaped. The horses and cows were killed; the swine, sheep, and goats were destroyed; the dwelling house, barns, and stacks of seed were burnt, the brew-house alone remained standing.

Almost everything at Vriesendael was destroyed except the house which DeVries himself occupied, a small fortress in itself. DeVries, no man to omit a chance to compare himself favorably with Kieft, said that his people at Vriesendael were saved in the very nick of time by the arrival of an Indian whom he had helped on the night of the massacre. This Indian told the other Indians that DeVries was a good chief, that he had helped him escape from the soldiers, and that he had tried to stop the killing of the Indians at Pavonia. The besiegers said they were sorry they had burned DeVries' buildings and destroyed his cattle; and that they would let his little brewery stand, though they wished to get the copper kettle to make heads for their arrows.

When spring came, the season for driving out the cattle, many Dutchmen wanted peace, and since it was time for the Indians to plant maize, they were equally anxious to stop the hostilities. After some negotiations, peace was concluded in May, 1643. Many doubted that it

* E. B. O'Callaghan (ed.), *Documents Relative to the Colonial History of New York* (New York, 1856), I, 190.

would be durable, and their doubts were quickly justified. At the end of the summer, as soon as their maize was ripe, the Indians again began to kill every isolated Dutchman they could find. Nothing was now heard but murders, most of which, the authorities were told, were committed under pretense of coming to put Christians on their guard.

In some manner the buildings at Achter Col had survived the first Indian attacks in the spring, though Johannes Winckelman, Myndertsen's agent, had been forced to evacuate the settlers to New Amsterdam, where he put them up at Philip Gerritson's city tavern at a cost of 132 guilders, 4 stivers. On September 17, 1643, however, the post was completely destroyed in a sudden night attack. "The house was set on fire, and the small garrison, 'five soldiers, five boys and one man,' after a determined resistance, finally escaped in a canoe, with nothing but their arms." A month later, the authorities reported that "the Indians swarm in that district and burn and slay whatever they come across."

Four soldiers stationed at the old Van Vorst farm at Ahasimus were murdered by nine Indians on October 1, 1643. The Indians, the report said, were so well disposed toward Jacob Stoffelsen, who now occupied the place, that they made a pretended errand and persuaded him to go over to the fort, and then, under the guise of friendship, when the soldiers had no arms in their hands, they killed them all, except Ide Van Vorst, the young son of Stoffelsen's wife by her former marriage. The farmhouse was set afire and the boy carried off to Tappan. DeVries later went to Tappan and negotiated his release.

Finally the Indians took the field and attacked the bouweries at Pavonia itself. Two ships of war and a privateer were there at the time and saved considerable cattle and grain. It was not possible to prevent the destruction of the bouweries, it was said, because they were burnt, not by open attack, but by Indians stealthily creeping through the brush and igniting the reed or straw roofs. Only the Van Vorst place, which was covered with plank, was preserved. By the fall of 1643, every other settlement in New Jersey had been destroyed.

The people of New Netherland, who had little enough use for Kieft before the war, now blamed him for the war and its outcome. Even Maryn Adriansen, the Hoboken plantation owner who had signed the petition which started the war and who had commanded the expedition that massacred the Indians at Corlear's Hook, turned violently against Kieft. Adriansen was probably not the most stable man in the colony after a brandy or two. Formerly a freebooter and seaman under a famous privateer, he had been charged with slandering the Director as recently as June, 1641, and with drawing a knife against the public prosecutor even more recently. When the owner of one of the burned houses upbraided him for his part in the Indian war, Adriansen concluded that Kieft, "seeing that the spit had fallen into the ashes," had been trying to shift the blame for the war to him. No man to let this pass lightly, Adriansen proceeded to the Director's house in the fort armed with a pistol, loaded and cocked, came unawares into the Director's room, presented his pistol at him, and said, "What devilish lies are you reporting of me?" Johannes de la Montagne, one of Kieft's councilors, jumped between them and let the hammer of the pistol fall on his thumb. Adriansen was immediately jailed. A short time later, when Adriansen failed to return home, Jacob Slangh, one of Adriansen's men, followed him to the fort, carrying a loaded gun and pistol. Slangh fired at the Director, but the ball hit a wall beyond him. The sentinel shot Slangh, and his head was stuck on a post as a warning to others. For his part, Adriansen was sent to Holland in chains, though he was soon back in America making trouble for the Company.

Those who saw that the evil of the war was too great for one man's shoulders, even Kieft's, piled the rest of the blame on the shoulders of the Company's only permanent civil servant, Secretary Cornelis Van Tienhoven, "a corpulent and thick-set person of red and bloated visage, and light hair, . . . a likely person, of ruddy face, corpulent body and having a little wen on the side of his cheek." Few men have ever had such articulate enemies as Van Tienhoven. They felt that no one could with truth say anything good about him or omit anything bad, and acted accordingly.

He gives anyone who has any business with him—which scarcely anyone can avoid—good answers and promises of assistance . . . yet he rarely helps anybody but his friends; but twists continually and shuffles from one side to the other. In his words and conduct he is rude, false, deceitful and given to lying, promising everyone and when it comes to perform, at home to no one.

They accused him of leading a young Dutch girl into an affair by promises of marriage on one of his official trips to the Netherlands, when he was a married man with a family in New Amsterdam. (Van Tienhoven complained that when he was arrested in Amsterdam, he was obliged not only to pay the fine but to provide some oysters and a drink for the two sheriffs, one of whom may have been Michiel Pauw.) He finally abandoned his wife and family in an apparently feigned suicide, when the Company began an audit of his books. No one in New Amsterdam ever saw him thereafter, though few believed that his hat and coat found floating in the North River marked his grave. The people's hatred for Van Tienhoven was a fair measure of their attitude toward the Company.

IV

PETER STUYVESANT AND THE
SECOND INDIAN WAR

In 1647, the Company appointed a new governor, Peter Stuyvesant, whose peg leg and colorful character have made him the very embodiment of New Amsterdam to later generations. Many Dutchmen had complained that the West India Company ought to send governors to New Amsterdam who were used to governing. DeVries told one official that he was surprised that the West India Company would send such fools into this country, who knew nothing except to drink, that they could not even be assistants in the East Indies, and that the Company by such management must come to naught. In the East Indies no one was appointed governor unless he had first long service and was found to be fit for it, but the West India Company sent, in the first instance, as superior officers, persons who had never had command in their lives. No one could complain that Stuyvesant was unused to governing or unwilling to do so. Before long the people of New Netherland were full to overflowing with government.

Peter Stuyvesant was born in the northern province of Friesland in 1610, the son of a minister of the Dutch Reformed Church. In 1632, he left the University of Franeker to become an employee of the West India Company. He probably worked for a few years at the Company's offices in Amsterdam, and for a time in the Company's colony in Brazil, and then was made chief *koopman* (commercial officer) in Curaçao, the Company's major possession in the West Indies, and soon became governor of Curaçao and two nearby islands. He lost his right leg in an assault on the island of St. Martin, one of the Leeward group which the Spanish had seized from the Dutch a few years before. In 1644 he returned to the Netherlands, and was fitted for the wooden leg he wore the rest of his life. He spent a year recuperating and was then named Director General of New Netherland.

Stuyvesant arrived in New Amsterdam on May 11, 1647, about three and a half years after the end of the 1643 Indian War. Few of the people he came to govern had moved back to the west shore of the Hudson, and those few had hardly ventured from the banks of the river.

New Amsterdam had prospered somewhat in the last decade. The church, it was true, lay half-finished and the fort was in its usual state of decay, and a quarter of the houses of the town were given over to petty trade, mostly tapping beer, wine, and spirits and selling tobacco. Its crooked streets were seas of mud when it rained, filled with wandering domestic animals whether it rained or not. Too often pigpens and chicken coops stood before otherwise respectable residences. Nonetheless, New Amsterdam was no mere trading post when Stuyvesant arrived. The town fairly breathed commerce. Among the large numbers of Dutchmen, Englishmen, Walloons, and Frenchmen in the settlement there were some few of all nations: Germans, Danes, Norwegians, Swedes, Finns, Portuguese, Spaniards, Jews, Italians, Czechs, and Poles. The burghers of New Amsterdam scorned the Yankees of New England for their diligence in pursuit of money, but if they themselves had any concern about the arts, letters, or learning it was kept carefully hidden from strangers. Everywhere, one visitor observed, the arrogance of Babel prevailed. Another complained of their sharp trading:

The people in this city, who are almost all traders in small articles, whenever they see an Indian enter the house who has any money, they immediately set about getting hold of him, giving him rum to drink. . . . If he should then buy anything he is doubly cheated, in the wares and in the price. He is then urged to buy more drink which they now make half water and if he cannot drink it they drink it themselves. They do not rest until they have cajoled him out of all his money, or most of it, or if that cannot be done in one day they keep him and let him lodge and sleep there . . . always managing that he does not go away before he has given them all they want. . . . When there are no Indians about, . . . they are constantly cheating and defrauding each other.*

In buying furs from Indians, a Dutchman's hand on the scales always weighed one pound; his foot, two.

As to religion, New Netherland was nominally Dutch Reformed, but besides the Dutch Reformed there were many English Puritans, many Lutherans and Baptists, and some Roman Catholics, Quakers and Jews. In the religious seventeenth century, many acted as if they had no religion at all.

It was a settlement with few of the amenities that softened life for Virginia planters and little of the mutual respect that made a hard life tolerable for New England Puritans. The ordinary people were, as Stuyvesant said, the scrapings of all countries, held together by few common ties, religious or patriotic, and, if they were wise, constantly on the watch against the greed, ambition, and overreaching of their neighbors, rich and poor. The government officials, for the most part, treated them as beneath notice until they came before the magistrates, which was all too often. Their contacts with the rich and powerful were few and seldom pleasant. Many were in fact on far closer terms with the slaves. They had little respect for authority, religious or secular, and little rea-

* Jasper Danckaert, "Jasper Danckaert's Journal," *Narratives of Early American History* (New York, 1913), 79.

⋘ 43 ⋙

son to have much respect for what they found of it in New Netherland.

The seventeenth century was a great watershed in the history of western civilization; it was an age of political and religious ferment and an age of great energy. Above all, it was the first great commercial age. Holland was reaping the rewards of the patriotic and religious heroism of the previous century, and few Dutchmen wanted to be called again to such high endeavors in the golden years that followed. New Netherland reflected it all. While the fur trade flourished, the settlement had many of the marks of the Klondike of a later century. Its people lived for the day and the hour. Few, of high or low degree, had any particular plan to go home; on the other hand, few had any vision of a permanent settlement in the New World.

The 1650's, however, began to see an influx of settlers who were neither browbeaten employees of the West India Company nor scheming Indian traders. By the time the English seized the colony, these men, Protestant refugees from France and the Spanish Netherlands, were coming in a stream, pressed by new religious persecutions abroad and by the threat of more to come. They, more than the first settlers of New Amsterdam, were the men and women who were to establish the character of Dutch New Jersey, though they were destined to live under Dutch rule hardly at all. The country west of the Hudson, in point of fact, was to be destroyed again before Dutch New Jersey, as later generations knew it, came to be.

The west shore of the Hudson, laid waste in the Indian War, had been considerably resettled in the past few years. Michael Jansen Vreeland had purchased Jan Evertsen Bout's Communipaw farm, including "a poor unfinished house and some few cattle," for 8000 florins, the main house and farm having been burned by the Indians during the war. Maryn Adriansen was back in Hoboken, where he had received a grant for 50 *morgen* of land. Jacob Jacobsen Roy, the gunner (constable) at New Amsterdam, bought land at the place which came to be known as Constable's Hook; Claes Carstensen, at Cavan Point, and Dirck Sieken (Dey), at Communipaw. Claes Jansen Van Parmarent, progenitor of the Jersey Dutch Cooper (Kuyper) family, had bought 40 *morgen* at Communipaw. For some forgotten reason everyone called him "*Jan Potagie,*" or "Soup John." Despite Indian opposition (the Indians had told Vreeland several times that they would fire his place again if he did not pay them something more for the land), at least ten tracts of 25 and 50 *morgen* were taken up on the neck of land nearest to Staten Island. Farms flourished at Hoboken, Ahasimus, Paulus Hook and Communipaw. Among the new settlers were Jacob Walingsen, the progenitor of the Van Winkles, who were to become famous because Washington Irving thought that a simple, good natured fellow of the name of Rip Van Winkle sounded better than the same fellow of some other Dutch name.

Cornelis Van Vorst, the founder of the celebrated Ahasimus bouwerie, had died in 1638. On March 31, 1639, the Company leased it to his widow, Vrouwtje Ides, for 20 years. Her second husband was Jacob Stoffelsen, born in Ziricksee, in Zeeland, in 1601, one of the earliest settlers of New Netherland, and the man who, as *werkbaas* of the Company's Negro laborers, had built the fort at New Amsterdam in the years between 1629 and 1635. The Ahasimus bouwerie had had a reputation for conviviality when Cornelis Van Vorst lived, but it became even more famous under its new master. Nothing in Van Vorst's day compared with Stoffelsen's entertainments, at one of which Captain Geurt Tysen, the famous privateer, sat down to a dinner where the guests consumed two entire sheep. (Captain Tysen, overwhelmed by this generosity, and the *brandewijn* that went with it, immediately presented Stoffelsen with a Negro as a token of his gratitude, at which Van Vorst's youngest son, feeling that since half of the sheep belonged to the estate of his father, half the Negro should also, brought the matter to court. The court, however, ruled in Stoffelsen's favor when he pointed out that two whole sheep from the estate had also been consumed at the young man's recent wedding festivities.) Tysen was not Stoffelsen's only acquaintance among the privateers nor was he the only privateer entertained at the bouwerie. In 1643, Stoffelsen invested 350 guilders in one of the expeditions of the privateer *LaGarce,* Captain Blauvelt and Anthony Coll, Masters, and sometimes kept valuable plate and other property safe for its officers when they were on the high seas. In 1646, when the *LaGarce* was refitted, Stoffelsen became one of her twelve owners. Many other privateers found the deepwater anchorage off Ahasimus preferable to the docks of Manhattan, where prying officials were underfoot at every turn. The good people of Pavonia and Communipaw were quick to point out that it was only the presence of a privateer in 1643 that enabled them to save their goods in the Indian War. For their part, they were not prepared to condemn all privateers because a few mistook a friendly ship for a Spaniard, or because a few others were slow to hear of any peace treaty that interfered with their trade. Who among us is without some fault? If the friendship of these good men brought them into disfavor with the officials on the other side of the river, they were quite used to dealing with the intrusions of those meddlesome fellows. Jan Evertsen Bout, Pavonia's first citizen, whose relations with a Negro girl in his service had come unfavorably to the notice of the authorities at New Amsterdam, was once obliged to tell the public prosecutor, *Fiscaal* Ulderich Lupolt, in plain Dutch, that he was *een hond, een dief, een schobbejack,* and that if he or any of his friends ever came back to Pavonia he, Jan Evertsen Bout, would shoot them, emphasizing his point by snapping his fingers in *Fiscaal* Lupolt's face.

* * *

On the morning of September 15, 1655, a large war party of northern Indians, about five hundred in number and heavily armed, landed on Manhattan in 64 war canoes. Stuyvesant and all the soldiers were a hundred miles away on the South River on an expedition against the Swedes. The Indians forced their way into the houses and moved about in the most threatening way, but made no open warlike move. They said they were on their way to attack their Indian enemies on Long Island. To the Dutchmen, their actions looked far more like the first maneuver in an attack on Manhattan.

About nine in the evening, after a day of tension, Hendrik Van Dyke, the *schout,* who was standing guard at his back gate, just south of where Trinity Church stands today, fired a blunderbuss at some Indians, killing a young girl among them. Some said the Indians were raiding his peach orchard at the time; others had it that he shot only after the Indians had wounded him in the side with an arrow. It was hard to put together any connected account of what happened during the day. At one time most of the able-bodied men were in the fort, where Cornelis Van Tienhoven was in command in the absence of his superiors. Van Tienhoven, who had been drinking brandy when the Indians first landed, began by trying to negotiate with them, but when they failed to go to Governor's Island by sunset as they promised, he ordered his men to attack. The Amsterdam Chamber later said the order had been given wantonly, "with clouded brains filled with liquor," but that pronouncement was made in the comfort and safety of the Company's offices in Holland. The Indians, who had themselves been drinking stolen liquor all day, were not to be removed by talk. Three Indians and two colonists were killed in the sharp skirmish which followed Van Tienhoven's order, and the Indians finally retreated to their canoes, but instead of going to Governor's Island, they crossed the river to Pavonia. It was not long before the people on Manhattan saw Maryn Adriansen's bouwerie at Hoboken in flames, and soon thereafter flames shot up from a dozen other places on the western shore. By morning everything at Hoboken, Pavonia, and Communipaw had been destroyed, and everyone who lived there had been killed or carried into captivity. Almost a thousand more savages then joined the first five hundred. After a day or two of terror on the west bank of the Hudson, they moved on to Staten Island and repeated the destruction there. In three days' time about fifty Christians were killed, more than one hundred, mostly women and children, were captured; twenty-eight bouweries and plantations and twelve to fifteen thousand *schepels* of grain were burned, and five hundred to six hundred head of cattle either killed or captured. More than two hundred persons lost all their possessions. Though the neighboring Indians of Ahasimus, Hackensack, and Tappan had but recently sworn eternal friendship for the Dutch, they were present with the others in the conflict and were guilty of shocking cruelties, murdering seven men and one woman in cold blood.

When Stuyvesant and the soldiers returned to New Amsterdam from the South River, the war ended as quickly as it started. Captain Adrian Post, who had himself been captured and released, was given the task of ransoming the captives from Pennecock, Oratany, and other sachems. Fourteen were released at Paulus Hook on October 17, 1655, and twenty-eight at the same place on October 21. For a time, Post was so busy ransoming captives that curiosity seekers had to be ordered not to cross the river and interfere with his work. Nevertheless, as late as March 28, 1656, the savages still held about twenty Dutch children.

When the Indian War was over, the good people of New Netherland went back to their usual occupation of complaining about the Company and attacking Director Stuyvesant. For its part, the Company had been in financial difficulties since 1645 and was wholly bankrupt after 1654. Many felt, so far as Stuyvesant was concerned, that his arrogance more than made up for his competence. They complained that everyone had to stand hat in hand while he sat with his hat on, peacock-like, in great state and pomposity, handing down arbitrary and capricious judgments on anything that came before him. People who had to tell him anything that did not please him were berated as clowns and bearskinners. The people lived like sheep among wolves, they said, not being able to speak to another without suspicion. One man wrote home in Latin: "Our great Muscovy Duke goes on as usual, with something of the wolf. The older he gets the more inclined he is to bite." Others complained that the officials of the Company contributed nothing to the colony but "arrests, imprisonments, banishments, confiscations, harsh prosecutions, blows, scoldings, reckoning half faults for entire ones and so forth; in a word, in ruining and estranging the country, offering everyone in particular who does not constantly please them as many insults as they can invent or think of . . ." Many said plainly that if their High Mightinesses, the States General, did not correct the situation quickly, there would be no chance to do so, for the English would annex New Netherland.

Nonetheless, the colony prospered under Stuyvesant's iron rule. Almost for the first time in its short history, its people could see a bright future before them. Immigration was increasing. As early as 1650 it was reported that if there were six times more accommodations or ships, they would all be filled. Within a few years, new settlers were coming by the hundreds.

V

COMMUNIPAW AND BERGEN

For a number of years after the 1655 Indian War, people were not allowed to live in unprotected outlying places, and the country to the west of the Hudson was abandoned to the Indians. Michael Jansen Vreeland, whose home at Communipaw had escaped the holocaust, removed himself and his family to the safety of Manhattan, where he kept a taproom. Several of the other refugees from Pavonia and Communipaw took up the same work. However, Peter Stuyvesant was not a man to abandon fertile land near peltry very long, particularly when it began to look more and more as if the recent Indian uprising was the last desperate fling of the savages near New York, as it proved to be. He soon opened negotiations with the Indians to repurchase Pavonia and Communipaw, and on January 30, 1658, bought all of the land south of Weehawken between the Hackensack and the Hudson. While he was carrying on his negotiations, Vreeland and six other "interested farmers . . . driven away by the savages from their farms in Pavonia, Gemoenepaen, and other neighboring places," told the authorities that they were inclined to reoccupy their former places of residence, to restore their buildings and to cultivate their former fields, but as they had been greatly injured and suffered immense losses by the incursions of the savages, they earnestly solicited an exemption from tithes and other similar burdens for a few years.

Their petition was granted on condition that they

group themselves in the form of a village of at least ten or twelve families, "to be in the future more secure for their defense . . . without which the Director General and Council deem the reoccupation of the deserted fields too dangerous."

Earlier, on December 31, 1655, Jacob Stoffelsen had asked permission to return to the Ahasimus bouwerie, pleading that he had twice been driven away by Indians and that he was now an old man of fifty-four. The officials insisted on their earlier orders against separate settlements, but let Stoffelsen return.

Vreeland and his six neighbors soon did the same. By June, 1658, Vreeland had enough cattle on his Communipaw farm to sell 27 head to the South River settlement. On the other hand, as late as October, 1659, one of the men on the west shore, Ide Van Vorst, was attacked by Indians while he was dressing meat and obliged to take to his boat and flee to New Amsterdam. (The authorities fined him for bringing meat to the city without an excise license.) In February, 1660, Vreeland and the others were admonished again to form a village, under threat of losing their property, but it is doubtful if they ever did anything about the admonition.

Twenty years later Communipaw was still a primitive place. Two visitors to the settlement slept upon some straw on the floor, and felt themselves lucky that their host sold blankets, some of which they used to cover themselves. After a hard night's rain, they could not find a dry place in the house to lie down. They had "some good cider, and enjoyed some roast raccoon, very fat and of good flavor." They had nowhere seen or eaten finer apples, they reported, very large, fair, and of good taste, only 56 of which could be put in a heaped-up bushel.

On March 1, 1660, Tielman Van Vleck, of New Amsterdam, and Pieter Rudolphus, a merchant of the same place, sought permission to settle on the maize land back of Communipaw, and were refused. Five months later the Director and his council reversed themselves and

Van Vleck and Rudolphus were permitted to found a village there, "on a convenient spot which may be defended with ease, to be selected by the authorities."

Van Vleck, who had studied law in Amsterdam, was descended from a prominent family of Maastricht in the province of Limburg, but he had lived in Bremen, Germany, for many years and was probably born there. He can be called the founder of the first town in New Jersey. The authorities chose a hill about two miles back of Paulus Hook for the settlement, a place about half way between the Hudson and the Hackensack, looking down on Mill Creek and the flatlands of Pavonia and Ahasimus to the east and the Hackensack meadows to the west. They called it Bergen. Bergen-op-Zoom, near Antwerp, stands on the same sort of hill, and some of Bergen's founders may have had the Brabant town in mind when they named it, but *"het dorp Berghen int nieuwe maiz lant"*—"the village of Bergen in the new maize land"—might well have borne the name if there had never been a Bergen-op-Zoom, or any other.

The village was laid out by Jacques Cortelyou, of New Utrecht, the colony's leading surveyor, much respected for his learning despite his Deist leanings in religion. He plotted Communipaw into village lots at the same time and was later to be one of the promoters of Acquackanonk, present-day Passaic. Two intersecting streets divided the village, an 800-foot square, with a small commons in the center and eight irregularly shaped lots in each quarter. He surrounded the whole with palisades set out a few feet from the ends of the 32 lots. Outside the palisades were about 27 more lots. One of them, on the south side of the road leading to Communipaw looking down over the flatlands below, was set aside for the church. A well was dug in the middle of the town square, with a long sweep to raise the water buckets, and troughs were placed around the well for cattle.

Founded just as New Netherland was at last surmounting its Indians troubles, Bergen flourished from the start. Though Paulus Hook and Communipaw were older and

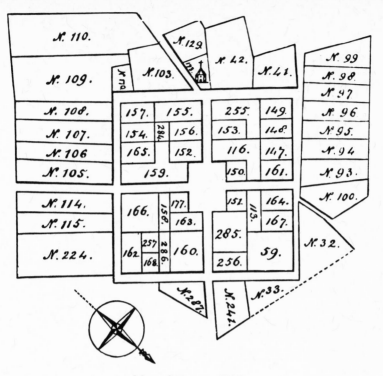

Map of Bergen, 1664
Winfield, "History of Hudson County"

closer to the river, and though both lay on the flat farm-
land so beloved by the Dutch, Bergen soon outstripped
them. Within a year, by November 5, 1661, it had a local
government and a court of justice of its own, with
Tielman Van Vleck as *schout* (sheriff-magistrate) and
three *schepens* (magistrates) to assist him, Michael Jansen Vreeland, Harman Smeeman and Caspar Steinmets.
All of the latter were probably residents of Communipaw
or Ahasimus, not of Bergen.

Smeeman, born in Westphalia 37 years earlier, had not
always been one of the colony's leading citizens. On
February 8, 1654, a Sunday, he was one of a crowd engaged in the loutish Shrovetide sport of riding the goose,
for which he was prosecuted. The object of the pastime,

which had once been popular in the Rhineland, was to seize the neck of a greased goose hung on a rope while riding rapidly under it on horseback, the riders usually having prepared themselves by drinking large quantities of liquor before entering the lists. Stuyvesant had often prohibited it, with little effect upon its devotees. "It is altogether unprofitable, unnecessary and censurable," Stuyvesant declared, ". . . to celebrate such pagan and popish feasts, and to practice such evil customs in this country, even though they may be . . . looked at through the fingers in the Fatherland." Vreeland, though a respected burgher about thirteen years older than Smeeman, was in no position to complain of his young friend, for he himself had made a considerable nest egg in two years of prohibited Indian trade near Albany in the 1630's, and had only recently been prosecuted for tapping after hours at his short-lived liquor business in Manhattan. (Vreeland confessed that two soldiers who were playing at backgammon and three sailors who were waiting for their skipper had their cans by them and got chatting, but he did not add that he had filled their cans against the time when he could not lawfully tap.) Steinmets, the third *schepen,* seems to have been more circumspect.

Bergen grew rapidly. All of its lots were soon taken up by prospective settlers, Sips, Tallmans, Van Winkles, Van Ripers, Marseleses, Van Buskirks, Edsals, Newkirks, Van der Lindes, Toers, Deys, Bayards, Zabriskies, Van Vorsts, Posts, and Van Vlecks, to name some of them. They lived together no more peaceably than other Dutchmen of the day; it was not long before *schout* Van Vleck was prosecuting Douwe Harmansen Tallman for calling Van Vleck's wife a vagabond, "and that at a time when Van Vleck was lying sick in bed." Communipaw, Pavonia, Ahasimus, Paulus Hook, and Pemrepogh (Bayonne, just north of Constable's Hook) and Mingagquy (the Greenville section of Jersey City) quickly became Bergen's dependent hamlets.

By 1662 it was large enough to ask for its own pastor, and a subscription was taken to support one, though none was available to serve. Engelbert Steenhuysen, a Westphalian, was named *voorleser.* Like the others of that honored but overburdened profession, he read a sermon on Sundays when no minister could come from Manhattan, led the singing of Psalms on every Sunday, taught school during the week, and filled in his spare time by cleaning the church and digging graves. Steenhuysen was highly aggrieved when, despite the custom of exempting schoolmasters, he was taxed like any other citizen because he was the owner of a house and double farm. He finally withdrew from the office.

By 1660, the trickle of immigration to New Netherland had become a flood. Some of the newcomers probably came because they saw that the opportunities in the New World were even greater than those in the prosperous Netherlands. Others, and by far the greater number, saw that the rise of Louis XIV of France was a deadly threat to religious freedom and self-government in Europe, in fact, a threat to every prospect of men of the middle class in the Old World. The Netherlands had been filled with these sturdy, self-reliant refugees from the ever-increasing domains of the reactionary king, men who had already felt the terror of the dragonnades in their home-lands. They were soon pouring into New Amsterdam on every boat, many from the Netherlands, some from refuges in Germany and elsewhere. New Jersey was to receive more than its share of them.

The Huguenot, David Demarest, whose descendants played so large a role in the settlement of the Hackensack Valley, was an example. Born near Amiens, in 1620, he and his family fled first to nearby Middelburg, in Zee-land; then to Mannheim, in the Palatinate, where he achieved considerable prominence; then to America. He arrived in New Netherland on April 16, 1663, almost at the end of the Dutch rule, on the *Bonte Koe,* which had recently been bringing immigrants by the hundreds. He went first to Staten Island, then to Harlem.

Men like Demarest were sturdy, self-reliant, and

deeply religious, but it would be a grave mistake to picture them either as ascetics or patricians. Like other seventeenth-century Europeans, they were earthy, aggressive men, who knew their rights and were quick to see any threat to them, real or imagined. They had not survived the terror of persecution by turning the other cheek, and they had no intention of turning their cheeks in the New World. The authorities probably soon wished that some of them had stayed at home. Demarest, for instance, was involved in a series of controversies with his neighbors in Harlem, in one of which he refused to pay tithes for the Dutch *voorleser,* because he was French and not Dutch, and carried on a long bitter litigation about it; having won that battle, he proceeded to move across the Hudson and join the Dutch Reformed Church. He was convinced that anyone who crossed him in any way was seeking his ruin, and he was prepared to defend his rights to the end against any interference. The men who opened the wilderness in New Jersey were men like Demarest; a century was to pass before their descendants took on the dignity of country gentlemen.

Aggressive as they were, there was a difference between these refugees and the Indian traders of earlier decades. The new settlers did not look back to Europe as home, or set themselves up in petty trade to get together a few guilders to return. Though indebted to the Netherlands for their escape from Europe, they had few patriotic ties to it, or to any other country of the Old World. The people of New England and the Virginia planters thought of themselves as transplanted Englishmen, but few of the recent arrivals in New Amsterdam considered themselves Dutch. Before many years, some of them, if asked, might have said that they were American. A shrewd observer would not have had to ask.

*   *   *

The story of the surrender of New Netherland to the English is quickly told. Four British warships, with more than a thousand fighting men, appeared in New York

Bay on August 26, 1664, threatened the fort with the guns of the fleet and the town with destruction by the soldiers. The Dutch authorities surrendered the colony. Peter Stuyvesant was almost the only man in New Amsterdam who was willing to defend it, and his superiors had given him no means to do so. Indeed, for months they had been ridiculing his espionage reports about the British threat to the colony.

The Dutch had no love for the English, but few tears were shed as the Dutch West India Company flag went down and the British flag was raised over the fort on September 8, 1664. If any Dutchman left the colony because it had become British, his name has been lost to history. Stuyvesant himself retired to his bouwerie north of town and most of the others went about their business as if nothing had happened. Some of their late descendants may look back to the golden age of Dutch rule in America; the burghers of New Amsterdam, as long as their conquerors were not Spanish or French, were not particularly concerned about it. Their attitude was in part a reflection of the unpopular rule of the Company and in part of their own narrow commercialism, but it also reflected the enlightened spirit of the seventeenth century.

*   *   *

In the last 40 years before the English conquest the Dutch had established a colony which was destined to become the greatest commercial center of the world, but for most of those years they set little store by it. They were in fact far more interested in privateering in the Carib Seas than in founding any colony at all. The Spaniards were drawn to America by the gold of the Indies and the call of their faith; New England was founded by dedicated men who believed they were raising up a new Zion on these western shores. Dutchmen, for their part, had been supported by little more than a feeling that it would be a mistake to let Spain take over the whole New World, that perhaps some good would come of a Dutch settlement there, that, in any case, it would be an adventure to try. The concepts of seventeenth-century Dutchmen were narrow and their efforts to carry them into execution were fumbling, and it is easy to see why political philosophers disapprove of the Dutch as colonists. Philosophers, of course, are not the men who open the wilderness.

The Dutch reconquered New Netherland on August 9, 1673, and held it for about a year, until the Treaty of Westminster, signed February 17, 1674, returned it to the English, but for all practical purposes Dutch rule in North America ended in 1664.

VI

THE END OF SWEDISH RULE
IN AMERICA

During the twenty years before the English conquest of New Netherland, New Sweden had a colorful
history of its own. The Swedes who lived on the east side
of the Delaware were a small minority, a mere appendage
of the more important Swedish settlements in modern
Delaware and Pennsylvania. There were 121 people in
New Sweden in June, 1644, but only 17 were on the east
side of the river, and all of them were soldiers at Fort
Elfsborg, near Varkins Kill, in modern Salem County.
The rest of the settlers were at Fort Christina, at the
Skyllerkill plantation, at the Upland plantation (Chester,
Pennsylvania), and at Tinicum Island, below modern
Philadelphia.

Though Governor Johan Printz knew that conflict
with the Dutch was inevitable, he followed his instructions and maintained peace with their garrison at Fort
Nassau, alternately flattering and insulting them, while
playing them off against the Indians and the English.
One Dutch protest, addressed to "The Honorable Rig-
orous Mr. Johan Printz," was thrown to the ground by
Printz with the contemptuous direction to an underling,
"There, take care of that." Printz then turned his back
on the messenger to talk to an Englishman, and when,
after a time, the man asked about a reply, Printz seized
a gun and tried to shoot him. Fortunately an aide threw
the Dutchman out bodily before Printz could aim and
fire.

Nonetheless, the Swedish position was precarious. Stuyvesant, in New Amsterdam, with ten times the resources of the Swedes, tired of the many complaints which came from the South River, twice had determined to go there, but each time he had been hindered. He then tried to overawe Governor Printz by sending a single vessel "with cannon and people well armed," but when Printz gathered his own small force, the Dutch officer, who had been ordered not to provoke hostilities, withdrew. Stuyvesant next took stronger measures. He himself marched across the country with 120 men, and arrived at Fort Nassau on June 24, 1651, where eleven Dutch ships (four well armed), which had sailed around the coast, met him. To impress the Swedes with his strength he cruised with his little fleet up and down the river, drumming and cannonading. The effect of this display was somewhat lessened when Printz manned his own little yacht with 30 men and followed the Dutch up and down the river. Neither side attempted anything of a hostile nature, contenting themselves with a paper war over the relative claims of their governments to the South River, and with efforts to strengthen their positions by purchasing Indian land titles. The Indians, who had little concept of land ownership, and, as one Swede said candidly, hardly any understanding of the difference between Hollanders and Swedes, were glad to receive whatever trifles the two sides offered, often for the same land, particularly since neither of them seemed to do anything about the places they purchased but give them strange guttural names which, the Indians soon learned to their astonishment, were supposed to be the Indian names for the places.

During these years, the Dutch had two forts on the river, Fort Nassau, built in 1626 within the limits of the present city of Gloucester, and Fort Beversrede, built in 1648 in the district now known as Passayunk, part of modern Philadelphia. Neither was very formidable. Almost as soon as Fort Beversrede was finished, the Swedes (perhaps emboldened by the fact that the Dutch had only six able-bodied men in both forts) erected a trading post within twelve feet of the gate and proceeded to amuse themselves by hacking away at the Dutch palisades and burning down Dutch fences nearby.

The Swedes' two forts, Elfsborg and Christina, were both more strategically located than Nassau and Beversrede. In the fall of 1651, Stuyvesant, unwilling to let such a situation continue, proceeded to move his cannon and military supplies downriver to a place called the *Santhoek,* several miles below Fort Christina, and to build a large fort, 100 by 200 feet in size and garrisoned by a substantial force, which he called Fort Casimir, at modern New Castle, Delaware. Printz, a contemporary Swedish historian explained, "either . . . had not the means of hindering it, or had not the time for it, and so the matter rested." Having countered the Swedes by out-flanking them, Stuyvesant went back to Manhattan in quiet triumph. The triumph was short lived. In May, 1654, the new Swedish Governor, Johan Rising, stopped the armed vessel on which he was coming to America at *Santhoek* long enough to seize the new Dutch fort. One of his officials wrote later:

The 21st of May, which was Trinity Sunday, we came to *Santhoek,* where we cast anchor and gave a Swedish salute before the Holland fort, which was erected and fortified on the land of Her Royal Majesty, the Queen of Sweden, through the violence of General Stuyvesant, Governor of New Holland, contrary to various protests from Governor John Printz; and nearby twenty-one houses had been built for the colonists.

[An officer] was sent with four files of musketeers to the Holland commandant . . . to demand the delivery of the said fort, and since they did not answer our salute from the fort, and also hesitated to give a verbal resolve, so in the meantime we let them have a couple of shots from our heaviest guns, over to the fort, by way of demanding an answer.

While the Dutch haggled for time to consider the matter, the Swedes occupied the fort, "took possession of their guns and cannon, removed the Holland flag and had the Swedish one brought from the ship and raised in its stead. . . . We called this Fort Trinity, because it was captured on Trinity Sunday." Rising's countermove would have been most effective to maintain Swedish supremacy on the river if it had not, as might have been foreseen, provoked Stuyvesant to drive the Swedes out of all the Delaware settlements once and for all.

The Dutch had been willing to play a game of move and countermove with the Swedes, but when the brash young governor, with no understanding of the rules, actually seized a Dutch fort merely because it was poorly defended, the Dutch were forced to take action, and probably most of the Swedes fully understood the situation. Almost a century later Peter Rambo, of Raccoon, told an inquiring traveler from Sweden:

> . . . the Dutch and Swedes had always lived on good, friendly terms with one another until a number of Dutchmen came and settled in New Castle, and until a ship arrived from Sweden that carried a captain by the name of [Sven] Scute, who had begun to shoot at the Hollanders to drive them away; this was the origin of the dissension between the two.

Under urgent orders from Amsterdam, Stuyvesant brought up a large fleet and a force of soldiers before Fort Casimir in September, 1655, and compelled a bloodless surrender. The Swedes, who were probably reconciled to the loss of the captured fort, were not at the end of their troubles. Stuyvesant proceeded to sail upriver and demand the surrender of Fort Christina itself, and after a few days of siege, that fort, and with it all of the Swedish possessions in America, fell to the Dutch.

The New Sweden Company had recently been showing great energy in sending out settlers and supplies. The ship *Mercurius* had left Sweden after the surrender, but before news of it arrived there, full of new settlers and with a hundred more clamoring for passage. After some bickering, the Dutch authorities let the passengers land, adding their numbers to the small Swedish settlement on the Delaware. Perhaps, given time, the Swedes could have built up a thriving outpost in America; more probably their efforts were doomed from the outset. The colony began in commercial rivalries among Dutchmen and never captured the imagination of enough Swedes to man even a few posts against a serious Indian attack. The Swedes in the seaboard cities at home were comfortable and content; the Swedes and Finns in the back country, who might have profited by emigration, probably could not imagine themselves undertaking such an adventure, if indeed they had ever heard of New Sweden.

Few of the Swedes in America were concerned over the end of New Sweden. Most of them considered their Swedish rulers arbitrary and oppressive and were willing to try Dutch governors in their stead. An old settler, half-Swede, half-Dutch, told Peter Kalm a century later that the Swedes "had been entirely satisfied under Dutch rule, he believed, because they had not heard anything for a long time from their mother country, nor received any aid from them and more particularly because the governor of New Sweden had been rather severe, and treated them mostly as slaves." (As to this report, Israel Acrelius observed, "though it was much talked about, it was probably groundless. . . . It is, however, probable that the Swedes, after they came into that Canaan and obtained a taste of a good hitherto unknown were now disgusted with such labors as were nothing to what was usual at home, and so conceived an unmerited hatred of their governor.") If Stuyvesant congratulated himself upon the Swedes' attitude toward Rising, he would have done well to restrain his joy. Within a few years his people were to prove no more concerned about his own troubles.

The Dutch occupation of New Sweden brought new life to the settlement for a time. In 1656, the Dutch West India Company transferred everything south of Fort Christina to the City of Amsterdam in settlement of a debt of twenty-four thousand guilders. Fort Casimir, renamed New Amstel, quickly took on new vigor. About a hundred new houses were built almost at once, and several hundred new settlers arrived, some of them from other parts of New Netherland. The Dutch considered settling some of their people on the east bank of the Delaware, but nothing came of this plan. "The condition of the land on the other side of the river was likewise good and fertile," the Director wrote home, "nor was it bad policy to begin a hamlet or village there," adding that it could not "do any harm to keep a strict watch here and there, so as to ascertain somewhat the intentions or actions of the Swedes."

The City of Amsterdam itself sent out a considerable number of settlers, among them some children from the Amsterdam almshouse, who were bound out to the townspeople. "Please to continue sending others from time to time," the Director wrote, "but, if possible, none ought to come less than fifteen years of age and somewhat strong." If children under fifteen years of age were troublesome, some of the other emigrants sent out by the city were even more so. The Director of New Amstel told the city fathers of Amsterdam that many of the people they had sent to the colony said openly that they would not put their hand to anything during the *blessed year,* as they called the year when they were provisioned from the City's store. The authorities urged the Director not to allow their good intent to be thus abused, no easy task for the Director. At the end of the Dutch occupation, though the City of Amsterdam had by then taken over all of the Company's holdings on the Delaware, things were little better.

When New Amsterdam fell to the English its outposts on the Delaware, including all of New Sweden, fell with it. Sir Robert Carr was dispatched with two frigates and hundreds of soldiers for the purpose. He seized New Amstel on October 11, 1664, a few weeks after the surrender of Manhattan, with some bloodshed and looting. The old Dutch magistrates were continued in their posts and anyone who wished to do so was allowed to depart from the river within six months. As at New Amsterdam, few if any seem to have been disturbed enough by the change in government to leave.

VII

EAST JERSEY

D UTCH NEW JERSEY hardly existed under the Dutch; it came into being under the rule of the English. Perhaps the new rulers were better suited to the new land; perhaps the English reaped where the Dutch had sown.

The end of Dutch rule in 1664 saw a few settlers living on the east bank of the Delaware, men and women of Swedish, Finnish, and Dutch extraction, the remnants of the New Sweden colony. A number of Dutchmen lived on the west banks of the Hudson at Communipaw, Pavonia, and Hoboken, and there was a promising three-year-old village at Bergen, a few miles west of the river. No Dutchmen lived in any of the other places we have come to think of as Dutch New Jersey. Hackensack, Acquackanonk (Passaic), Schraalenburgh (Bergenfield and Dumont), Second River (Belleville), English Neighborhood (Ridgefield, Leonia, Englewood), Harrington, Old Tappan, Tenafly, Paramus, Pompton, Totowa, Fairfield, Preakness, the Monmouth County country, New Brunswick, Raritan (Somerville), Neshanic, Millstone, Three-Mile Run (southern New Brunswick), and Six-Mile Run (Franklin Park) were all wilderness, almost unknown to white men.

At the end of Dutch rule, there was nothing in New Jersey that would be recognized in the twentieth century as a Dutch house; indeed, there were few houses that even a Dutchman of the seventeenth century would have acknowledged as Dutch, and there were no churches at all, Dutch or any other.

The last few years of New Netherland had seen many Dutchmen move themselves across the Hudson to the village of Bergen, and the same spirit soon led them to seek new homes even farther away. In fact, to an amazing degree, the men and women of Bergen, who had hardly finished roofing their crude houses there, were the very people who went out to the new lands along the Passaic and the Hackensack.

The first moves into northern New Jersey were made, however, not by Dutchmen, but by English settlers from the New Haven colony and Long Island. At first glance it seems a perfectly natural thing that when New Jersey had become English, Englishmen would want to settle there. In point of fact, the opposite was true. Many people of the New Haven colony, unhappy with their neighbors' encroachments and the turn of events in England, had been planning to move to New Netherland for years. They probably would have preferred the old Dutch rule to the rule of the cynical court favorites of Restoration England, but many of them refused to let the change of government alter their plans and founded Newark, Elizabethtown, and Woodbridge despite their doubts about John, Lord Berkeley, and Sir George Carteret. They soon discovered that court favorites did not make bad rulers. Men like Berkeley and Carteret wanted little from their proprietorship but money, and New England Yankees (and Jersey Dutchmen, for that matter) were old hands at dealing with money problems. They were quite used to people who wanted money, and very little of theirs ever found its way to England; indeed, most of them were soon going about New Jersey as if they had never heard of Proprietors. Before long the Proprietors abandoned the losing battle to rule such people, and turned the government over to the Crown.

With the country beyond Newark Bay opened by these English settlements, and Indians no longer a serious threat, the valleys of the Hackensack, the Passaic, and the Raritan became attractive indeed, and land speculators patented most of the land there as soon as the Proprietors threw it open for purchase. The Hackensack Valley will serve as an example. By 1669, thousands of acres had been patented by William Sandford, Nathaniel Kingsland, John Berry, Samuel Edsal, Philip Carteret, Robert Vauquillan, Samuel Emmett, Isaac Bedlow, Balthazar De Hart, James Bollen, and others. These men, most of whom were close to the proprietors, hoped to resell the land to Dutch farmers, though Berry, Edsal, some of the Kingslands, Sandford, and perhaps others became settlers themselves. Their hopes of attracting Dutchmen were not disappointed. Within ten years the patentees had sold most of their land to the Van Buskirks, Bogerts, Van Emburghs, Westervelts, Bantas, Leydeckers, Paulisons, Brinkerhoffs, Mandevilles, Van Nordens, Sloats, Van Horns, Vreelands, and Van Houtens who were to people the valley in the next hundred years. The Demarests, Smiths, Zabriskies, Blauvelts, Harings, and others patented their own land, and the Loziers, Duries, La Roes, Alyeas, Christies, and others came with them.

Dutch New Jersey was settled by men and women from the other Dutch settlements in America, New Amsterdam, Brooklyn, Harlem, and Long Island, seldom if ever by colonists from Europe. In the Hackensack Valley, the Brinkerhoffs, one of the earliest settlers in Old Hackensack (Ridgefield Park, Bogota), came from Brooklyn. The Van Buskirks, who took up the New Hackensack tract (Teaneck) were from Bergen, and their fellow purchasers, the Bogerts, Westervelts, Bantas, and others came from New York, Brooklyn, or Bergen. The Zabriskies were from Bergen. The people of the French tract (New Milford, Bergenfield, Dumont) were almost wholly French Huguenots from Harlem, though one, James Christie, was a Scottish schoolmaster who may have come there directly from Aberdeen. All of them were drawn to New Jersey by its cheap, fertile land and its ready water communication with New York City.

For the first ten or twenty years, the people of the Hackensack Valley made the day-long trip to Bergen by boat or Indian path to go to church and to have their

David Demarest House, erected New Milford c. 1686
Fred Van Dyke

children baptized. In 1686, a church was organized at
Old Hackensack, and in 1696, when John Berry gave the
church a tract of land in New Barbadoes (modern Hackensack), it was moved there. The communities of Schraalenburgh (Bergenfield, Dumont) and Paramus (Ridge-
wood, Hohokus, Waldwick, Paramus) also grew up
around Dutch churches, which had been founded there
because they were convenient to the neighboring farm
country. Within fifty years, travelers found one farm next
to another for miles north of the Hackensack meadows,
the whole, as one of them put it, one small town. The
same pioneer spirit had carried many Dutchmen well up
into the mountainous country at the edge of the New
York highlands and into the New Jersey mountains to
the west, many of them men and women with the same
family names as those of the lower Hackensack Valley.

View of Aquackanonk
J. W. Barber and Henry Howe,
"Historical Collections of the State of New Jersey"

The case was much the same in the Passaic Valley.
There, the Acquackanonk Patent was granted to 14 purchasers in 1682. The patent followed much the same
course as others, a grant to enterprising speculators and
quick settlement by Dutch farmers: Van Ripers, Posts,
Vreelands, Spiers, Garretsons, Van Winkles, Van Houtens, Marinuses, Van Giesens, Jurianses, Doremuses, and
others whose names have been bound up with the
Passaic Valley ever since. In this case, most of the Dutchmen who planned Acquackanonk came from Bergen and
Communipaw and moved to the settlement themselves,
drawn again by the fertile bottom lands along the river.
It was not long before the whole valley was filled with
Dutch farms. In 1759, an English clergyman who traveled
from Newark to the celebrated falls of the Passaic, was
amazed at the rich country, covered with fine fields and
gentlemen's estates, which he saw along the Passaic River.

The country along the Raritan was settled later than
the Hackensack and Passaic valleys. (As early as 1652,
Cornelis Van Werkhoven, a political figure of importance
in Utrecht, had arranged to buy land in the Raritan
Great Meadows and in and around Kill van Kull, but

after some controversy in the Amsterdam Chamber, he abandoned his purchases.) In June, 1681, an Englishman, John Inians, and others bought about ten thousand acres at the point where the Indian path to the south crossed the Raritan, in modern New Bruswick, and the nearby country soon filled with Dutchmen, most of whom were from Long Island: Voorhees, Terhunes, Strykers, Lotts, Amermans, Cornells, Fishers, Montagnas, Sebrings, Schencks, Van Arsdales, Vanderbilts, Van Cleefs, Van Dykes, Van Nuys, Williamsons, Vanderbergs, Vrooms, and Patersons. Some Dutch settlers in New Brunswick came from as far away as Albany; indeed, the people who lived on Albany Street were reputed to hold themselves above other people in town.

The Dutch also settled Freehold and Middletown, on the Navesink. They told the Amsterdam church authorities in 1730:

> . . . for more than thirty years now, divers families have come from time to time from New York to take up their abode in this adjoining province of New Jersey. Many have also come from Long Island to the Navesinks. . . . At first they were ministered to by the preachers of Long Island, who, by turns, at certain fixed times of the year came over for this purpose. But it was too difficult for them to continue to do this, and also not without peril, on account of the great bay they had to cross, and the considerable distance. For they made the journey in a small vessel and under fierce winds.

A nearby Scottish minister, "who had not a perfect mastery of the Dutch language," served for many years on a part-time basis, but they now sought their own preacher from Holland.

The Dutch settlements along the Hackensack, the Passaic and the Raritan traced back to New Amsterdam, Long Island, or Bergen. There was another Dutch settlement in New Jersey with wholly different antecedents, in the area called Minisink, on the upper reaches of the Delaware River, separated from the rest of the Dutch

The Village of Hackensack c. 1800
Courtesy of the New York Historical Society

country by a hundred miles of trackless forest and by a formidable range of mountains.

The Minisink settlement was an appendage of Esopus (Kingston) on the Hudson River, one hundred miles overland to the northeast. Indeed, it was said that the authorities at Philadelphia did not know of the Dutch settlements along the upper Delaware until 1727, when they sent a surveyor to visit the Minisink Valley and see who the Dutch settlers were and what they were doing there. What the surveyor found could hardly have been more astonishing to him if he had come upon the legendary sailors of Henry Hudson playing bowls. The local people told him:

Not very long after the landing of the first colonists at New Amsterdam, some of the more enterprising determined to penetrate the country in search of minerals. With this purpose they followed the course of the Hudson, northwards as far as Esopus . . . where they landed and explored west-wardly, through the Mamakating Valley, for about fifty miles. Here they discovered a mine of lead ore. Encouraged by this success, they continued their explorations, and about fifty miles further on they found traces of copper which soon proved to be abundant and valuable. This was on the Dela-ware River where the mountain nearly approached the lower point of Pahaquarry Flat.*

One very old man, Samuel Dupuis, had lived on the New Jersey side of the Delaware for many years. He had a grove of apple trees of a size far beyond any grown near Philadelphia. Dupuis told the surveyor that when the rivers were frozen he had a good road to Esopus, some one hundred miles from the mine holes, on the mine road. He took his wheat and cider there for salt and necessaries, and did not appear to have any knowledge of where the Delaware River ran or of the Philadelphia market.

Sixty years later, in 1787, Nicholas Dupuis, the son of Samuel, was living in a spacious stone house in great plenty and affluence, near modern Shawnee, Pennsyl-vania. The old mine holes were a few miles above on the Jersey side of the river, at the lower point of Pahaquarry Flat, below Millbrook. Before the boat channel was opened down the Delaware, he and his neighbors used to drive loaded wagons to Esopus on the mine road several times every winter. He could give only traditional accounts as to when and by whom the mine road was made or what the ore was that they dug and hauled on it. He had heard from older people that in some former age a company of miners came from Holland, who, they supposed from the great labor expended in making the road, were very rich. There were two mines, one at Paha-quarry Flat, the other about half way between the Dela-ware and Esopus. He had heard that large quantities of ore had been hauled on the road but never could learn

* John W. Barber and Henry Howe, *Historical Collections of the State of New Jersey* (Newark, 1844), 507.

whether the ore was lead or silver. In 1787, there appeared to have been a great deal of labor done on the Pahaquarry Flat mine holes at some former time, but the mouths of these holes were full of caved-in rocks and overgrown with bushes. General James Clinton, who had been a surveyor under his father while the latter was Surveyor-General of New York, and Christopher Tappan, Clerk of Ulster County, both of whom knew the mine road well, were united in the opinion that the road was built while the State of New York still belonged to Holland and that it undoubtedly must have been the first good road of that extent ever made in any part of the United States. Little more of the history of the road and mine holes has ever been found.

Among the Dutch names in the settlement were several well enough known in Esopus: Van Campen, Westfall, Westbrook, Schoonmaker, Depue, Cole, and Mandeville, but none of them seemed to have any tradition that their own ancestors had worked the mines. The dates of their

Southwest View of Deckertown, c. 1840
J. W. Barber and Henry Howe,
"Historical Collections of the State of New Jersey"

arrival in the Minisink settlement are fairly well authenticated as being after 1680.

The country was full of Indians, but a Dutch family named Decker had established themselves some miles across the mountains to the east; indeed, surveyors for the West Jersey proprietors as early as 1715 found a fairly large number of Dutch and German settlers all along the disputed New York-New Jersey provincial line. Whatever their origins, the men and women of New Jersey's Minisink region were to live for a century on one of the most dangerous frontiers that ever existed in America, under constant threat of Indian attack during the French and Indian wars and the Revolution, and under constant threat of violence from across the province line during the New York-New Jersey border wars.

In most of Dutch New Jersey there is no record of any conflict with the Indians after the 1655 Indian War. Though the Indians who lived at Ahasimus, and the Hackensacks and the Tappans, had joined the Mohicans in 1655 when they destroyed the Dutch settlements in New Jersey, they were essentially an agricultural people who were not given to fighting unless provoked. They moved back quietly to the frontiers as Dutch settlers filled up the country in and around Manhattan Island. David Godwin, whose father (a distinguished patriot during the Revolution) settled on the banks of the Passaic, at the site of modern Paterson, in the 1770's, wrote of one Indian tribe that had once lived near Communipaw, moved to Totowa, and later to the Minisink country:

After the Indians left Communipaw they settled at Totowa, on the now-called Bergen County side of the river . . . on a piece of woods selected by them for their wigwams, back of which they had their burying ground, a mound raised perhaps eighteen inches or two feet above the level of the land which I often crossed, even after the war. My father, then living in New York . . . had a wish to locate somewhere in the country . . . went to Totowa, where he seemed satisfied to settle. He made known his intentions to the chiefs of the Indians; they were much pleased. He then returned to New York, made known his intentions to my mother, who consented to go with him, though in a wilderness. . . . Father commenced building a small house [near the southwest corner of present-day River and Bank Streets, in Paterson]. As soon as he had finished enough for his family he moved them there. . . . About the time father commenced building over the river, the Indians found their hunting ground got to be too public, and concluded to move back. The chiefs went and selected a spot on the river at Minisink, there they moved, though the parting with them and the inhabitants was very hard. They had lived in the greatest harmony for years. The chiefs would come back every spring and fall to Totowa and bring as much venison, young bears and wild turkeys and small game as would last half of the inhabitants for a week. This they kept up for some time after, and while they were at Totowa, whenever father went from home, they would not leave mother alone. I have heard her say they would take my little brother with them to their wigwams to play with their papooses and return him in the evening loaded with their little trinkets, particularly with a little papoose, perfectly ornamented with wampum and porcupine quills dyed in the most splendid colors.*

The widening settlements of the Jersey Dutch can be traced in the Dutch Reformed churches, beginning in Bergen in 1660, spreading to Hackensack, Acquackanonk, and Tappan about 1690, to the neighborhood of New Brunswick about 1700, to Six-Mile Run about 1710, to Schraalenburgh, Paramus, Readington, and Fairfield about 1720, to Totowa, Clarkstown, New York, and Neshanic about 1750, and to Kakiat, New York, Bedminster, and Millstone about 1770. Each new church marked the opening of a new frontier, and as the country became settled the churches marked the boundaries between the Dutch settlements of New Jersey and those of their English and German neighbors, for in good degree the country which makes up Dutch New Jersey will be found within a radius of five miles of these churches.

* William Nelson and Charles A. Shriner, *History of Paterson and its Environs* (New York, 1920), 276.

To perhaps a greater degree, the lives of the Jersey Dutchmen in the years that preceded the Revolution centered on the same churches. At times when religious concern was at its height, many a Jersey Dutchman spent most of his waking hours thinking about things of another world—in sharp contrast indeed to the things that occupied the minds of his recent forebears in worldly New Amsterdam. The Calvinist doctrine of election, so distasteful to many modern minds, placed before religious Dutchmen of the 1700's one of the noblest hypotheses that men have conceived: that the great Sovereign of the universe had, in His goodness, elected some (hopefully themselves), sinners though they were, to be saved in the holocaust of sinners to come. Men so embued were not concerned with the petty things of life; they lived moral lives as a matter of course and looked forward to the day when their new American Zion would overcome the evils that had plagued the world from its foundation.

The renewed interest in religion was not without political implications. The Glorious Revolution of 1688-1689—the revolution that deposed James II and put William and Mary on the throne of England—had unleashed a furious conflict in New York which touched deep political and religious emotions. In many ways the conflict foreshadowed the Whig-Tory division of the American Revolution; the ordinary people, under the leadership of Jacob Leisler, violently supported the revolution abroad; the aristocrats either held aloof or opposed it. When the revolution succeeded and James was driven from the throne, the people of New York expected that its opponents would be punished and its supporters rewarded. Instead, the aristocrats who opposed the revolution succeeded in convincing the new governor, a weak and foolish man, that Leisler's party, not theirs, was the enemy of William and Mary, and persuaded him to hang Leisler and one of his aides as traitors, though they had been the very men who had held the colony for William and Mary while the aristocrats were doing everything they could to frustrate Leisler's efforts. This monstrous miscarriage of justice had a profound and lasting effect on the people of New Netherland, largely alienating the Dutch middle class, and in particular the French Huguenots, from the aristocrats of the colony, mostly men close to the royal government, and those with any similar pretensions. The cleavage in the Dutch Reformed Church was even sharper. Ministers like Henricus Selyns and Rudolphus Varick, who took the side of the aristocrats, lost most of their hearers. Before the Leisler affair, Varick had been coming from Brooklyn twice a year to preach at Hackensack. After Leisler's execution he was told that Hackensack's churchpeople could do very well without ministers and that he was not welcome. As a result, the few ministers who spoke for the people took over the real leadership of the American Dutch Reformed Church. It was a searching experience, one which could easily have set the Holland Dutch and the French Huguenots against their English rulers. Instead it left them committed more deeply than ever to their rights as Britons and deeply resolved to maintain them, and more deeply than ever committed to their Calvinist religion.

Three ministers were preeminent in the upsurge of religion in Dutch New Jersey that followed. One of them, Guiliam Bertholf, owed his very elevation to the ministry directly to the Leisler affair. Bertholf, a cooper from Sluis, in Dutch Flanders, a zealot of the despised Koelmanist sect of the Dutch church, came to America in the hope of becoming a school teacher or *voorleser*. He found a place as *voorleser* in Harlem, where he became a prominent supporter of Jacob Leisler during the "rebellion." As a result of the misguided actions of the established ministers in supporting the aristocrats, the people of Hackensack and Acquackanonk paid Bertholf's way back to Holland to be ordained a Dutch Reformed minister, perhaps somewhat irregularly, by a South Holland *classis*. The protests of Amsterdam and New York meant nothing to him or his people, and he went on to a long and successful ministry, becoming the founder of almost every early Dutch church in New Jersey. Dr. T. J. Wertenbaker has said:

Casting aside all formalities, he went from one isolated community to another, preaching, teaching, praying, and organizing. We find him now on Staten Island, founding the church at Port Richmond, now he is on the east bank of the Hudson at Tarrytown, now he is deep in the New Jersey wilderness organizing the church at Ponds, now he is preaching at Harlem, now at Tappan.

Neshanic Dutch Reformed Church, c. 1756
Fred Van Dyke

Not only did he become the real founder of the Dutch church in New Jersey, he instilled into it an evangelical spirit which bore little resemblance to the formal religion of the state church whose name it carried.

"Perhaps then it was not a matter of chance," Dr. Wertenbaker continued, "that the congregations on the Raritan called as their first pastor Reverend Theodorus J. Frelinghuysen, a brilliant young minister tinged with the doctrines of the German Pietists." Frelinghuysen took Dutch farmers, concerned with little but baptism, marriage, and burial, and made saints of them against their wills. His methods were forceful, almost outrageous. He threatened, abused, and cajoled them, and made bitter enemies of many. On one occasion, when administering communion in the church at Six-Mile Run, he cried out, as he saw the communicants approaching the table, "See! see! even the people of the world and the impenitent are coming, that they may eat and drink judgment to themselves." Several returned to their seats, and many more were incensed. Frelinghuysen's insistence that people show some deep religious experience before calling themselves Christians made many Dutchmen feel that he was robbing them of their religion. The Amsterdam authorities could do nothing to stop him. Like an Old Testament prophet, he seemed to care not at all that his hearers were offended at him if they understood his message. In the end he won over most of his enemies, and it has been said that his spiritual influence continued on the Raritan for a hundred years after his death. Like Bertholf, he was accused, and perhaps not without cause, of being less Dutch Reformed than Labadist or Koelmanist.

The third was John Henry Goetschius, of Schraalenburgh and Hackensack, a man of the same spirit. Short of stature and short of temper, making enemies wherever he went, the young Swiss minister, who had started to preach as a circuit rider in the Pennsylvania wilderness at seventeen, brought the Hackensack Valley to the same religious concern that Frelinghuysen had preached on the

Raritan. He was one of the principal founders, over violent opposition, of Queen's College, now Rutgers University. His theological students were the men who became the leaders of Dutch patriot sentiment in New Jersey and New York when war came; his students were the men hunted down by the British as teachers of rebellion; his enemies were the men who became the willing supporters of Toryism among the Dutch. His spiritual influence, too, continued for decades after his death.

Some historians have believed that the revivals of religion under Bertholf and Frelinghuysen were the beginnings of the religious awakening that swept all of the colonies in the two or three decades preceding the Revolution. Whether they were or not, they were important among the forces which changed Dutch New Jersey from a fur trading wilderness to the settled, prosperous farm country of the 1770's.

The religious awakenings of the early eighteenth century affected one and all. whether they were descended from fur traders or Huguenot refugees. Even those who considered themselves unmoved by religious fervor would have been thought religious to a fault by Wouter Van Twiller and the Dutchmen of the 1620's. As a student of the period has said, thousands were given a new view of life's values, which gave direction not only to their lives but to the development of the whole American people, a spiritual drive which stimulated every charitable, educational, and progressive movement, and Jersey Dutchmen were in good degree transformed by it.

Of course, not all of the Dutch Reformed ministers were Bertholfs. Dutchmen suffered under many men who were unsuitable for their tasks. Some had nothing but contempt for the wild ways of America, and wished they were back in Holland. Rudolphus Varick, who occasionally served at Bergen and Hackensack before the people there turned to Guiliam Bertholf, told Amsterdam that ministers in America would soon have to live on their own fat. Cornelius Blauw preached at Pompton Plains,

Northeast View of New Brunswick, c. 1840
*J. W. Barber and Henry Howe, "Historical Collections
of the State of New Jersey"*

Totowa, and Fairfield, and later at the irregular church at Hackensack and Schraalenburgh. His people complained that he preached only one day in the week. "Some say that he gives himself up to greediness, and serves his own belly. . . . He has become so fat that he is almost too lazy to move himself." Domine Gerardus Haeghoort, at Second River, though a learned man, stirred up trouble wherever he went. Many others succumbed to the drinking habits of the day.

*   *   *

The Dutch colonial church is a distinct mark of Dutch New Jersey, though "Dutch" is perhaps something of a misnomer, for no structures like Jersey Dutch churches existed for a hundred years after the end of Dutch rule in New Jersey. Dutch churches are more English than Dutch in their design; and the people who built them, though they spoke Dutch and were Dutch Reformed in denomination, were as likely to be named Zabriskie or Froeligh or Christie or Berry or Lozier as Van Dyke or Van Norden or Westervelt.

There was no church building of any kind in New Jersey in 1664, and there were only three or four in all of New Netherland. The first Dutch church in America, the church in the fort at New Amsterdam, followed Dutch medieval tradition in its style. It was the only one to do so. Most of the early churches in New Netherland were octagonal, in the style which Killiaen Van Rensselaer directed his agents to follow in Albany: "It ought not to be a very complicated matter," he said, "the shape being mostly that of an eight-cornered mill." The design was popular among Calvinist churches abroad as well as here, and among the German Reformed as well as the Dutch, its severely plain, utilitarian style being suited to the Calvinist tenets against outward show.

Octagonal Church at Hackensack, 1696
B. Spencer Newman

Many such Dutch Reformed churches were built on Long Island and elsewhere in New York. The first Dutch church in New Jersey, the Bergen church of 1680, followed the octagonal form, as did the Hackensack church of 1696, and possibly the Paramus and Schraalenburgh churches of about 1724. Englishmen, unaccustomed to the style, likened them to lighthouses, "only occupying more ground at the base." Others thought they looked like large haystacks with pointed roofs. After a time, a belfry was built on the Hackensack church by the church-masters, Dirck Epke Banta and Joost DeBaun, "which has here been recorded in their praise," as the church records noted. At Six-Mile Run the second church, built about 1766, "was a [square] wooden building en-closed with shingles and painted red, with a white front, with a roof terminating in the center, on which was a low steeple, having a cock for the vane." The church at New Brunswick and the church at Tappan were also square buildings, severely plain with the four-sided roof receding to a central belfry. The square church built in Harlingen "was in the ancient style of Dutch architec-ture, with high gables and steep roof, an aisle at one side, from which a door opened; along the sides were short pews for the men, while the body of the church was di-vided into small squares, occupied by chairs for the women and children." In both square and octagonal churches, the men sat on benches around the wall and the women sat in rows of chairs in the center, with the bell rope falling into their midst, and the high pulpit, backed by a large sounding board, was at the wall oppo-site the door. None of the octagonal buildings stand today, nor do any of the small square or nearly square buildings which supplanted them.

The sandstone churches we have come to know as Dutch colonial are of the same style as the English Pres-byterian churches of middle Jersey and, though plainer in detail, in the same style as the Anglican churches of New York City. The Bergen church of 1773 (no longer standing) was among the first of these church buildings, the Hackensack church of 1791 the next. The South Schraalenburgh and Paramus churches of 1799, the North Schraalenburgh church of 1801, the Millstone church and others followed quickly. No one, however,

South Schraalenburgh Church, Bergenfield. Erected 1799; enlarged 1868

Fred Van Dyke

could mistake any of them (save perhaps the Millstone church, with its gleaming white weatherboarding) for an English church. Their studied avoidance of architectural embellishment shows too clearly that their builders were proud to be plain Dutch, even when they were abandoning the church architecture of their fathers. Though few in number, the Jersey Dutch churches have seemed to many prejudiced Jerseymen to be the epitome of American colonial church architecture.

The Jersey Dutch contribution to American life which is easiest to identify is the Dutch colonial house, an architectural style which reached near perfection in the early 1800's in the valley of the Hackensack, in Bergen County, and nearby Rockland County, New York. Many examples are found in all of the Jersey Dutch country, where their beautiful proportions and quiet charm have stood for two centuries, reminders of a dignified, God-fearing, and self-respecting day that is gone, and an unheeded reproach to the Victorian gingerbread houses, the California bungalows, the miscalled "colonial" houses of the 1920's, and the split-levels of the 1950's which have sprung up like weeds around them.

The buildings we know as Jersey Dutch farmhouses are a native design. The style has been said to have no prototype in Europe, though some writers think it was derived from the Flemish cottage of Belgium east of the Scheldt, southern Zeeland, and the northern tip of France, where the flying gutters and floor plans of the peasants' cottages suggest possible models.

In 1664, at the end of Dutch rule in America, there were no houses of the style which we now call Dutch colonial. The city houses of that day were like those of Amsterdam or Delft, with a gable end facing the street as the most conspicuous feature. Only a few Dutch farmhouses showed any influence of this style, and none, so far as is known, was built in Dutch New Jersey. When the Dutch first came to America they probably dug square pits in the ground, lined them with timber and roofed them with sticks and bark. In fact, Cornelis Van Tienhoven himself recommended that course to new settlers many years later:

Those in New Netherland . . . who have no means to build farm houses at first according to their wishes dig a square pit in the ground, cellar fashion, six or seven feet deep, as long and as broad as they think proper, case the earth inside all around the wall with timber, which they line with the bark of trees or something else to prevent the caving in of the earth, floor this cellar with plank and wainscoat it overhead for a ceiling, raise a roof of spars clear up and cover the spars with bark or green sod so that they can live dry and warm in these houses with their entire families for two, three or four years, it being understood that partitions are run through these cellars which are adapted to the size of the family.*

The first houses were little better than these dugout shelters. When Minuit and a shipload of emigrants reached Manhattan on May 4, 1626, they found a log blockhouse under construction at the lower end of the island. During the following summer and autumn they built nearly thirty houses of unpeeled logs, thatched with reed, on the west side of the island above the unfinished fort. They also began a counting house of stone for the Company and two windmills, one for sawing lumber and another for grinding corn. In 1628, when the population of the Manhattan settlement had reached 270, the residents, an official reported, were beginning "to build new houses in place of the hovels in which heretofore they huddled rather than dwelt."

At that time the barn and dwelling house of the peasants of southern and central Holland and nearby Germany were combined in one building. The back part was for the cattle, which stood in rows on either side, with a large open space in the center, called the *deel,* where the carts were kept. A large arched double door led into it, while the thatched roof came down low on either side. Leading from the *deel,* or stable, into the living room was a small door, with a window to enable the inhabitants to see what was going on among their friends of the

* E. B. O'Callaghan (ed.), *Documents Relative to the Colonial History of New York* (New York, 1856), I, 368.

fields. For a time the farmhouses of New Netherland closely resembled these peasant houses. A typical house, built in the Harlem settlement in 1638, was 42 by 18 feet in size, with a stable and threshing floor in the rear; the cows, horses, and sheep occupied the low areas under the roof on the sides, and the family lived in the smaller quarters in front. Nine hundred bundles of reeds were used for the roof. The style survived to a degree in the high-roofed Dutch barns of later periods. By 1650, the living quarters were usually separated from the barn and stable, though they provided little more room for the family. These houses were small one-story structures, often with a low rough stone wall five or six feet high and a steep roof without overhanging eaves. They had few and small windows, stone fireplaces or ovens, and chimneys of boards plastered inside with mortar or mud, with little more than a hint of the later architecture that was to be called Dutch.

By this time, the more prosperous people in New Amsterdam itself were living in quite substantial houses. With the Company's large sawmills turning out planks and timbers for export, most of them were built of wood, but there were enough brick houses with their colorful gable ends to remind Dutchmen of home. Many were two or three stories in height by 1647, with stepped, straight, or graceful curved gables which would have done credit to a burgher of Edam or Leyden. Though Dutchmen would have preferred the tiled roofs of home, long after a kiln was opened, in 1628, roofs, eevn on Manhattan Island, were still being thatched with reeds.

The Dutch gambrel roof, perhaps the most distinctive feature of the Dutch colonial style, did not come into being until the beginning of the eighteenth century, long after the Dutch occupation. Though the gambrel roof was known in Europe, and in New England and Virginia, where it had considerable popularity, the Dutch roof, with its upper slope of about 23 degrees, a break, and then a lower slope of about 45 degrees extending to a wide flaring bottom, is found nowhere else in the world.

House of Benjamin P. Westervelt, Cresskill.   Erected c. 1730;
enlarged 1808

Fred Van Dyke

It is a combination of slopes and curved overhanging
eaves which has been called the most beautiful gambrel
known.

Where the Jersey Dutch lived close to English neighbors, two-story houses were built; elsewhere one and one-
half stories were the rule, despite the large Dutch families
of the day. Brick and wood were sometimes used, but
native sandstone is the characteristic material, quarried
on the property or in a nearby field, shaped with dull
axes in the early days and later sawed with stone-saws,

mostly with slave labor. In the case of rough stone, every second row was brought to a level with smaller pieces of stone, these level-lines producing an appearance of solidity that adds much to the charm of the style. Many of the later houses were large substantial structures, carefully finished inside with carved woodwork and tiled fireplaces, reflecting the wealth and prominence of their owners. The Dirck Dey house at Preakness, the Vreeland house at English Neighborhood, the Huyler and Westervelt houses at Tenafly, the Hopper house in northern Paramus, and the Van Dyke house at Kingston remain as charming examples. The houses are not unique to New Jersey—they are found on Long Island and in the Hudson Valley as well—but by far the greatest number are in the valleys of the Hackensack, the Passaic, the Raritan, the Millstone, the Pequannock, and the Ramapo: treasures of which the State of New Jersey can well be proud.

The Dutch barns were equally distinctive. With the doors at the gable end and low walls at the side, hardly high enough for the hinder ends of the horses and cattle which stood there, no observant traveler could confuse them with the barns of the nearby Englishmen, where the wagon entrance was on the long side and there were high walls on all four sides. The Dutch "hay barrack" also differed from the English haystack. It consisted of four heavy poles planted in the ground, with a sliding four-cornered roof which could be raised or lowered as the hay supply grew larger or smaller. Many houses had separate kitchen outbuildings, with huge stone ovens, some of which survive as relics of the days when slaves served the people in the big house nearby.

Jersey Dutchmen did not stop moving into the wilderness when they reached the banks of New Jersey's rivers. New Hackensack in Dutchess County, New York, settled in the late seventeenth century, did not get its name by chance. Large numbers of Dutchmen from the Raritan Valley and the Hackensack Valley went to Gettysburg,

Pennsylvania, and Boonesboro, Kentucky, in the 1760's and for some decades later, and many Jersey Dutch Tory refugees fled to Nova Scotia, New Brunswick, and Ontario at the end of the Revolution. No one who knows the Jersey Dutch will wonder where the name Van Horn, Texas, came from, or Sebring, Florida, or Zabriskie Point, in Death Valley, California, or who were the ancestors of people named Brouwer, Van Riper, Van Winkle, Amerman, or Voorhees, wherever they now live.

VIII

SWEDISH SETTLEMENTS IN
WEST JERSEY

F EW SWEDES moved to the east side of the Delaware for
many years after the English occupation of New Sweden
in 1664. The New Jersey side of the river was originally
regarded as a wild land, where nothing would thrive, and
old settlers reported that almost forty years passed before
anyone felt disposed to settle and establish a home there.
The first settlement was said to have been at Gloucester,
"where the Hollanders had their Fort Nassau," Matts
Mattsson probably having been the first to build a house
there. Settlers who thought that the east side of the river
was wild land soon discovered their error. Peter Lind-
strom, an engineer and surveyor who had come out with
Governor Johan Rising, reported as early as 1653 that
the land between Salem Creek and Repaupo Creek was
"entirely fertile and suitable for tobacco plantations,
and beautiful and rare fruit trees, with fine pasture land
and many beautiful valleys, and fine streams which ran
up into the country."

Once the first settlements were made in New Jersey,
other settlers followed. By the time of the English conquest, the Swedes on the Delaware, like the Dutch on the
Hudson, were beginning to see that the Indian trade
offered no future, and were giving it up and becoming
farmers. As early as 1668, three of them, Cornelius Lear-
son, Ole Rasen, and Ole Jonsen, patented a tract of land
comprising all of modern Gloucester County, and they

passed their rights on to others; Hans Hopman, Peter Jonsen, and Juns Justasen, who "seated and improved upon ye said land" as early as 1673; and Ole Dircks, Will. Bromfield, Juns Justasen, Lasse Anderson Colman, Hans Hopman and his two sons, and Peter Freeman, Mans Justasen, and Paul Corvorn (the spellings are those of the English clerks) were owners of part of the tract by 1677.

A small settlement near Salem brought the people, mostly Finns, into quick controversy with Major John Fenwick and his large Quaker colony, which had been established at Salem in 1675. That doughty man, who saw West Jersey more as a solution for his towering load of debts than as a refuge for the Friends, with whom he quarreled as much as with anyone else, vigorously denied having any connection with the English government at New Castle or New York, claiming to be "subject to no man but God and King." Fenwick once went to the house of one of the Swedish settlers, Gillis Giljansen, and demanded that he come to Salem and acknowledge Fenwick's proprietorship, threatening anyone who paid a tax to the New Castle authorities with the loss of his lands. He was not without grounds for his claims, but the rights and wrongs of his conflicts with the government would be hard even for Englishmen to assess; doubtless few Swedes wasted any time in pondering them and hoped only for peace under their new conquerors. At the very time when Fenwick was disputing the land questions with the Swedes, an English ship arrived on the Delaware with 230 additional colonists for the Salem settlement. They spent that winter at the Swedish village of New Stockholm, at the mouth of Raccoon Creek near Repaupo, the hospitable Swedes being so crowded by the newcomers that some of them had to lay their beds in cow stalls.

Fenwick died in 1683, shortly after William Penn acquired the chief interest in the West Jersey proprietorship. The Swedes lived thereafter in the greatest harmony with the Quakers during the whole colonial period, for though the Swedes' pastors were much offended at what they considered the informal, not to say disorderly, religion of the Quakers, the Swedes themselves were soon so intermixed with their English neighbors that one could hardly distinguish the Swedes from the English.

A Swedish minister, writing in 1693, gave a very graphic picture of the situation of the people in the Swedish settlements of that day:

> We are almost universally farmers, who plow and sow and practice agriculture, and live according to the laudable old Swedish customs in meat and drink. This country is also very rich and fertile land in all kinds of grain, so that, God be praised, it bears richly and abundantly whatever we sow and plant in it, so that we have plentifully our support in meat and drink. . . . We live in great amity with the Indians, who have not done us any harm for many years.

The founding of Swedesboro, the principal Swedish settlement in New Jersey, is a tale in itself. The Province of West Jersey laid out a highway from Burlington, the

Swedesboro (Raccoon) c. 1840
J. W. Barber and Henry Howe, "Historical Collections of the State of New Jersey"

capital, to Salem in 1681. By 1703, the King's Highway was completed as far south as Raccoon Creek, in the center of the Swedish settlements. These settlers had become increasingly restive about their treatment by the Swedish church authorities on the other side of the Delaware, and the completion of the new highway and the arrival of a vigorous new preacher, Lars Tollstadius, fresh from a controversy with the church authorities across the river, stirred their enthusiasm to build a new church on the banks of Raccoon Creek near the site of the new highway bridge.

There is little historical evidence less trustworthy than the complaints of the orthodox against the unorthodox, and no one will ever know whether Lars Tollstadius was a colorful adventurer or a dedicated man of God. He came to the Delaware Valley in 1701 without any authority from the Swedish Consistory, claiming to be a minister. The aging Andrew Rudman, pastor of the Gloria Dei Church at Wicacoa, however, was glad to make him his assistant, and allowed him to preach and catechize children, but not to administer the sacraments. In March, 1702, a new minister, the Reverend Andreas Sandel, who had known Tollstadius abroad and had told him to keep out of the Swedish settlements if he came to America, arrived as Dean of the Swedish churches in America, and ordered him out of the country. Instead, Tollstadius moved across the river to join friends living along the Raccoon and Mantua creeks. Sandel relented enough to tell him that he could instruct children there as long as he did not preach, an order which Tollstadius ignored. He began within five or six weeks, Sandel complained, "to preach here and there, scattered the people, and excited them against their good teachers, so that if [anyone] came to that quarter to preach, he had but few ears." There is no reason to think that the resulting controversy was conducted on either side with any excess of Christian charity. For most of the Swedes of New Jersey, the errant young preacher was a Moses in the wilderness. The pastor of the church at Christina could

storm that the decreased revenue would further impover-
ish him; they would yet have their church. Ten acres of
land bordering Raccoon Creek were bought in the fall of
1703. In June, 1705, before a rude altar, in a log building, the self-styled pastor was at last able to ascend his
own pulpit and preach one of the lengthy sermons so
much in vogue at the time. The new church was a
declaration of independence of the New Jersey Swedes
from their fellows in Pennsylvania, and was to make
Raccoon, now Swedesboro, the principal center of Swedish settlement in New Jersey.

The settlement was never dense. Travelers between
Raccoon, Penn's Neck (modern Churchtown), and
Repaupo found single farmhouses scattered here and
there, with the country far more forested than cultivated,
the roads, most of the time, running through the woods.
Thinly settled as this country was, many Swedes and
Finns pushed even further into the open frontier to the
east.

Eric Palsson Mullica, born in Halsingeland, Sweden,
in 1636, had come to America in 1663, after Swedish
rule had ended, and moved to New Jersey about 1697.
His children spread themselves widely from the Delaware to the Atlantic Ocean, where the Mullica River,
the Mullica Inlet, and the town of Mullica Hill perpet-
uate the family name. There was a considerable Swedish
settlement at Port Elizabeth on the Maurice River, and
there were scattered settlements as far away as Cape May.

In 1764, when the Reverend Carl Magnus Wrangel
and the sheriff of Gloucester County made a week-long
trip to the coast, they found many Swedes among the
people who were working in the lumber trade in the
heavily forested country along the way. At the Blue
Anchor Inn, about thirty miles from Gloucester, the
proprietor was an Englishman and his wife a Swede, both
old friends of Wrangel from Raccoon. The people
thereabouts made their living by making boards, timbers and cedar shingles, which they shipped to Philadelphia on the small rivers. Ten more miles brought the

travelers to the Egg Harbor River, where there were more docks for loading timber, and they spent the night at the home of a Swede named Carl Steelman, where the multitude of deer antlers hung as trophies on a high fence surrounding the house told one and all that a mighty hunter lived there. Steelman was born in Raccoon, and his wife was the daughter of a Long Island Dutchman who had moved to the neighborhood of Egg Harbor River fifty years earlier. They were much concerned that their eight children knew nothing of Christianity, and sought Wrangel's help as a teacher. An old Swedish couple named Streng, who had once lived in Raccoon, and an eighty-five-year-old brother, were particularly glad to see a Swedish minister again, for they spoke only Swedish in their home and still used Swedish books in their family devotions. Others were living almost as heathens, Wrangel felt, and almost the only Swedish custom which was being observed was to have the neighbors gather for three or four days of eating, drinking, and dancing whenever there was a wedding, without much thought of piety.

Wrangel and the sheriff then went on several miles to the seaside, where their host, an Englishman, took them to the home of still another member of the Steelman family. Sounds of music came from the house when they approached, and they found most of the people drunk, and at least one of the guests (the schoolmaster, in point of fact) in an argumentative mood, insisting that his drinking was an innocent pastime. Wrangel's Anglican host said that what they had seen was the customary behavior of people thereabouts, that those who disapproved were looked upon as fanatics and hypocrites.

At their next stopping place, Little Egg Harbor, twenty miles away, they found a thriving town, with more than twenty vessels tied up at the docks, ready to carry off lumber and flour as far as the West Indies. The owner of the principal mill, a Presbyterian, had built a small wooden church. Most of the Swedes evidently worshipped there, but Wrangel was distressed to find at least two Swedish brothers, "now gray-haired, [who] lived as absolutely savage heathens in cabins in the woods . . . providing for themselves by hunting and spending everything they earned on rum . . ," who were completely disinterested in his preaching. When Wrangel tried to speak to one of them about the next world, he was turned off with the somewhat cryptic observation that in a tannery you find as many hides as heads. The next day the travelers went on to see the ocean. They rowed out to a long narrow island, which protected the mainland from the breakers and the cold winds of the sea, where they caught masses of oysters and crayfish, saw horseshoe crabs, whose shells were used as scoops in the boats, and shot wild geese, gulls, and other birds. They landed on the island and crossed it to the ocean side, where they drank of the salt water, reputed to be so healthful that people with all kinds of ailments came there in the summer to bathe in it and drink it. Wrangel collected a big pile of mussels, snails, and shells, and watched the sandpipers, who caught insects in rhythm with the waves, a most entertaining sight, and slaked his thirst with wild grapes. He and his companions caught fish, and shot many feathered creatures, and after four hours returned with a rich supply of food. Some of the Swedish Kyn family also lived near the coast, one of whom, John Keen, is said to have owned the island Wrangel visited (now Atlantic City) as early as 1734.

*   *   *

When the Swedes and Finns began to move to the east side of the Delaware, in the late seventeenth century, they spoke Swedish and lived in low log houses, and, if they had a horse, were happy to ride on a crude saddle and behind a crude sled in winter, an old Swede told Peter Kalm in 1740.

The houses which the Swedes built when they first settled in New Jersey were very poor, consisting of one little room, the door of which was so low that one was obliged to stoop in order to get in. As they had brought no glass with them, many were obliged to be content with little holes, before which a moveable board was fastened. The chimneys were made in a corner, the ovens for baking were likewise inside.*

Before long some very substantial log houses were built. The home erected on Tinicum Island (just below Philadelphia) for Governor Printz in 1644 was two stories high, of hewn logs, with an interior made of finished lumber and fireplaces made of bricks imported from Sweden. The pastor's house, erected in Swedesboro in the 1720's, and many houses of other well-to-do farmers in New Sweden of the same period, were of the same general style, and by the time of the Revolution the Swedes' houses were indistinguishable from those of the English settlers.

The change from windowless log cabins to Georgian brick houses was but outward evidence of the transforming effect of the prosperous New World on the rugged Jersey Swedes.

The country, one minister wrote home, overflowed with every blessing, so that the people lived very well without being compelled to too much or too severe labor. Farmers, he said, lived much as they did in Sweden, but they were clothed as well as the well-to-do townspeople at home, adding that there were no poor in New Sweden, that no man who would labor would suffer want. "As soon as a person is old enough, he may marry in these provinces without any fear of poverty," another wrote. There was so much good land yet uncultivated that a newly married man could get a spot of ground without difficulty where he could comfortably subsist with his wife and children. "The liberties he enjoys," the writer said, "are so great that he considers himself as a prince with his possessions."

All of this put heavy strains on the Swedes' rugged virtues and on their ties to the old country, and as a result, during the next hundred years, the people of New

* Adolph B. Benson, (ed.), *Peter Kalm's Travels in North America* (New York 1937), I, 272.

Sweden largely cast off the ways of the Old World and took on the ways of the New, despite every effort of the older people to hold to the old Swedish ways. It was a particularly sharp blow to the Swedish Lutheran ministers who had been sent to America; articulate and learned Europeans, they were saddened to see the Swedish language, Swedish respect for authority, and Swedish willingness to endure poverty and hardship disappear. These men wrote of their troubles with much feeling—the change meant the virtual end of their ecclesiastical authority, as that authority was known abroad—but not without a certain admiration for the undisciplined, self-confident, self-respecting, and self-sufficient Americans their people had come to be. In the 1750's, Israel Acrelius felt that the fifty years preceding his ministry had seen the end of most of the Swedish virtues.

Formerly, the church people would come some Swedish miles [about six English miles] on foot to church; now the young, as well as the old, must be upon horseback. Then many a good and honest man rode upon a piece of bear skin; now scarcely any saddle is valued unless it has a saddle cloth with galloon and fringe. Then servants and girls were seen in church barefooted; now young people will be like persons of quality in their dress; servants are seen with *perruques du crains* and the like; girls with hooped skirts, fine-stuff shoes, and other finery. Then respectable families lived in low log houses, where the chimney was made of sticks covered with clay; now they erect painted houses of stone and brick in the country. Then they used ale and brandy, now, wine and punch. Then they lived upon grits and mush, now upon tea, coffee and chocolate.*

The dignified Swede of the 1750's, he said, could no longer clothe himself according to the weather; it would expose him to ridicule to wear skins or furs. They talked of their forefathers who used to do so, but laughed at them. To ride in a sled was considered ridicu-

* Israel Acrelius, *History of New Sweden, or the Settlement on the River Delaware,* W. M. Reynolds (ed.), (Phila., 1874), 310.

lous. In the summer men and women dressed in linen as light as decency would permit.

The new prosperity also had a leveling effect. "Here almost everyone is of the same stamp. Many a one goes and plows who is the owner of one or two hundred thousand *dalers*," Reverand Nicholas Collin was amazed to find on his arrival in 1770. Even chimney sweeps and street pavers were called gentlemen and ladies, and he had often come into a house and seen ladies sitting there barefooted at their tea. "If things were on the same footing in Sweden," he observed, "many a hungry stomach would not rumble under a silk vest." Despite this new dignity and affluence, Collin was obliged to add that the Swedes always managed to find great difficulty in supporting a minister.

Some of the Swedes felt the changes keenly, particularly the loss of the Swedish language. Acrelius reported:

The old among our people do not speak English well, can hardly read an English book or clearly understand English preaching; and, in a word, they hate in their hearts everything that is English. They say that they are Swedish people, although they are in an English country. Some of the young people have learned both languages, and bring up their children in the same manner.

By the time of the Revolution, there were said to be "only about two hundred persons who partly speak and understood Swedish." In many families, the father or mother could speak Swedish, but not both, and in such cases few of the children understood more than a word or two of the old language. When Carl Dalbo died in 1773, though he was a warden of the Swedish church and one of the best of Swedes in the opinion of his pastor, none of his children could understand Swedish, much less speak it.

The Finnish and Dutch languages had long since suffered the same fate. "Some families originally Dutch have long been regarded as Swedes," the Reverend Nicholas Collin noted in 1786, "since they have learned the

Swedish language and some of them can still speak or understand it." Åke Helm, of Raccoon, told Peter Kalm in 1749 that his father, one of the first settlers, told him that the Finns had never had a clergyman of their own, but had always had themselves served by the Swedes, that they had always spoken Finnish among themselves, that most of them settled at Penn's Neck, where there were people who until very recently had spoken Finnish, but that by 1749 most of them were dead and their descendants changed into Englishmen. Some of the Swedes would not admit a knowledge of Swedish lest they be thought backward. On a journey from the Maurice River to Cape May in 1750 Peter Kalm had a Swedish guide along who could not himself speak Swedish. There were many such of both sexes, he said, for since English was the principal language in the land, all people gradually got to speak that, and they became ashamed to talk in their own tongue, because they feared they might not be considered real English. Many Swedish women were married to Englishmen and, although they could speak Swedish very well, it was impossible to make them do so, for when they were spoken to in Swedish they always answered in English. Kalm felt that this doomed the Swedish language to extinction in America.

The greatest bulwark of Swedish sentiment was, of course, the Swedish Lutheran Church, and it was the greatest sufferer as the old ways disappeared. The Swedish authorities at home continued to send ministers to the congregations on the Delaware until a few years after the Revolution, although, once in America, the local people paid their salaries, or that part of their salaries which they received. The clergymen who came to America soon discovered the difference between serving a wealthy state church in Sweden and a frontier church in the New World.

There may be some truth in the suggestion that a large percentage of the Swedes were actually Finns, who resented the efforts of Swedish clergymen to force the Swedish language on them, and that both the refusal of some of the people to speak Swedish and some of the troubles of the Swedish church traced to that cause. Though Finland had been part of Sweden since the twelfth century and Swedish civilization had largely supplanted the Finnish, the two peoples differed widely in character and appearance, the Swedes being the most Nordic of people and the Finns of the same stock as the Magyars of Hungary. Some were said to excel in the black arts, and Printz had to imprison two of them for practicing their magic in New Sweden. "Karin, the Finnish woman," had worked at Fort Elfsborg, and may thus be regarded as the first of her profession in New Jersey. A competent Finnish sorcerer could always raise the wind. He tied three knots in a string. When he untied one, a strong breeze blew. When he untied the second there was a gale. No record exists of anyone who ever dared to untie the third.

Penn's Neck, which was largely Finnish, may have reflected some of the Finnish disaffection. The Sinnickson family, the wealthiest and most prominent there, had not only lost the Finnish language of their ancestors, but refused to talk Swedish. Pastor John Wicksell found it almost impossible to get the congregation to repair the Penn's Neck church.

. . . Both gable ends were . . . entirely opened and broken down, there were no windows, and the roof on the sunny side was absolutely rotten. . . . With what danger and difficulty divine worship was held in this open hen house the first two winters . . it seems best here merely to mention.

He listed only six women and four men (a Swede, a Finn, a Dutchman, and an Englishman) as regular communicants of the Swedish Lutheran Church in 1741. Though they later changed their minds, in 1742 the Penn's Neck congregation told their pastor that "no Swedish services should be held any more in the church of Penn's Neck, but all was to be English, with prayers and ceremonies according to the Church of England."

Probably few of the Swedes were as outspoken as the Indian who is said to have wandered into the Swedish church at Raccoon, looked about him, and after listening a while, said, "Ugh, a lot of prattle and nonsense, but neither brandy nor cider," and went out again. Nevertheless, there is much evidence that the pastors found many people indifferent or hostile. The congregation in Christiana, across the river, talked for years about the old times, when, if the minister found anyone hostile to him in the church, he took him by the arm and put him out of the door. "For a long time, when one went to church, nothing was to be expected at the church door but quarrels and maledictions between the minister and his people . . . for a long time, also, no parish meeting could be held without being broken up by dissension before it had well begun." The minister who could not overcome evil with good, Israel Acrelius observed, had better seek a place in another land.

At the request of the German Lutheran congregations at Cohansie (Friesburg), Pastor Johan Wicksell conducted services for them once a month on a weekday and occasionally on Sunday, since "he understood German fairly well and lived only eighteen miles away at Raccoon." He threw himself into the work with zeal, but he soon found himself in the center of a controversy among the local people about building a church. It is described in some detail in the journal of the Reverend Henry M. Muhlenberg, the distinguished German Lutheran clergyman. Pastor Wicksell, he said, was very partial to a certain refined, courteous "chirurgeon," Dr. Bodo Otto, a Prussian who lived at Raccoon, whom he considered very useful, and whom he wanted to be president of the little church council. Since Dr. Otto lived 18 miles away, in another town, many of the congregation, among them Jacob Fries, who was giving the land for the church, opposed the suggestion. This sorely offended Pastor Wicksell, and on his next visit he preached on the text, "Woe is me that I sojourn in Mesech . . ." and in his application, in somewhat broken German, he drew an angry, exaggerated parallel between Mesech in the Orient and Fries in the Occident. He insulted everybody, using somewhat unscriptural expressions in doing so. Mr. Fries and Mr. Wicksell had words about the sermon in front of the church after the services.

On his next visit, the pastor delivered no sermon, but came down from the pulpit and read a harangue, in which he repeatedly called Fries names and insulted him with cutting, libelous remarks which made some of the listeners laugh and offended others. Some weeks went by, and friends arranged a meeting for a reconciliation. It ended quickly. Mr. Wicksell flew into a rage, grabbed Fries by the front of his waistcoat, shook him, called him a liar, and ran out of the house pouring out abuse. Mr. Wicksell's next and last visit to Friesburg was even more memorable. Mr. Fries had sent over two quarts of wine for communion service. After the preparatory service was over, the preacher dismissed the people from the church and remained there alone with the chirurgeon. When the people were called back, the deacon came to Fries and asked for the two quarts of wine. Fries replied, "I have already sent two quarts." The deacon answered, "Whoever has guzzled it, we must still have two quarts for the communicants." Fries brought the wine. During the communion service, Mr. Wicksell threw off his coat and administered it in trousers and shirt; after the service, while he was quarreling and finding fault with Fries, the parishioners said he smelled strongly of garlic and wine. The earthly remains of Mr. Fries now lie by the Friesburg Church, where he was buried in 1806.

In 1744, many of the Swedish congregation at Raccoon became so disaffected with their ministers that they "allowed themselves to be seduced into departing from the pure Lutheran doctrine . . . to the Moravian," and an entire set of new trustees and church wardens had to be chosen. The Swedish church in America also suffered from undisciplined adventurers who took advantage of the freedom of the new land to show their indifference to church order and rules. Some were earnest men, who opposed order and rules because they thought such things stood in the way of devotion to God; others were doubtless restless spirits who merely found them inconvenient.

The Swedish Lutheran minister who best understood America and Americans was brought down to defeat by men of forms and rules, complacent men who would not bend an inch to the New World. The Reverend Doctor Carl Magnus Wrangel, though a member of the Swedish nobility, was far closer in temperament to Frelinghuysen, Goetschius, and Muhlenberg than to many of his colleagues. He saw the futility of the orders of the Swedish church authorities to use the Swedish language when only a few of his people understood it, and began to use Anglican prayer books in English; he saw the hunger of the country people for a religion that went beyond church attendance and forms—and was denounced by his fellow ministers as a revivalist and recalled to Sweden for his trouble. "He was one of the most popular preachers the Swedes ever had among them, and was usually obliged, on account of the crowds who attended his ministry, to preach in the open air," one of the historians of New Sweden wrote in the early nineteenth century. Wrangel came out well enough in the end: he became preacher at the Swedish Royal Court when he returned home. The victory of his enemies, on the other hand, was dearly bought. The American congregations soon told the Swedish authorities to send no more ministers unless they were asked to send them, and they were never asked. By 1800, the Swedish churches were all Episcopalian. The success of the enemies of Bertholf, Frelinghuysen, and Goetschius would have produced the same result among the Dutch Reformed.

Some of the Lutheran pastors were perhaps too scholarly for the rough-and-tumble New World. Israel Acrelius and Nicholas Collin, who served at Swedesboro, were among the most learned men of colonial America, but if they had hoped that their fellow Swedes would show great respect for their learning and pastoral advice, they were disappointed.

Nicholas Collin, the best known of the Swedish clergy-

Trinity Church, Swedesboro. Erected 1784; completed 1791;
steeple added c. 1825

Fred Van Dyke

men, a graduate of Upsala, who lived for many years
among his people at Swedesboro, found them and their
neighbors most exasperating. Beset by Quakers, Moravians, Methodists, Baptists, and Presbyterians, who all proclaimed a religion of experience that appealed to simple
back-country folk, he maintained his forms and procedures as if he were pastor to a congregation of country
squires at home. Unused to the heat and mosquitoes of
the lowlands along the Delaware, he nonetheless drove
himself to the point of breakdown in parish duties which
would have daunted a circuit-riding Methodist. He conducted his services first in Swedish and then in English,
often accompanied by open quarrels between the two

factions as to which should be used. Some insisted on a baptism service in Swedish even though no one but the pastor could understand it; others refused to be present if a word of Swedish was spoken. Collin complained that most of his people were poor and indifferent to religion, at least until they needed his services at a wedding or a funeral. Yet he left at Swedesboro, as a testimonial to their generosity and his own good taste, one of the most beautiful church buildings in early New Jersey—a building, it will be observed, not in the Swedish style, but in the best English Georgian style of the day. He was even more critical of the Quakers and Presbyterians of South Jersey than he was of his own people. Diligent and faithful to his religion to the point of martyrdom, he nonetheless lacked any warm understanding of the new land.

Good and evil are mixed in a queer way in this free country. Many who diligently make use of the clergyman's services contribute little to his support; others again, less fervent, and sometimes those who can hardly be considered parishioners, are more liberal, and in other matters more honest minded. The real Swedes are generally no better than others, neither in religion, morals, nor friendliness toward their pastors.

He complained that American children often obtained what they wanted through insistence and noise, and were allowed to do and act as they wished. He seldom mentioned an instance of immorality in his journal without observing that such things were common in America; he considered the tanned look of Americans unhealthy; he found Americans to be selfish lovers of gain. (Swedes, he felt, were laudably ambitious.) He particularly warned educated Swedes against coming to a land where their talents would be unappreciated. He found American girls passable, but the Swedish ladies, to his mind, "possessed great preference to these, both in bodily and spiritual advantages," adding however that he would not be so unreasonable as to deny that America possessed excellent women. Remarking upon the early loss of their teeth, he told a friend that he feared that he would have to chew for any wife he took in America. In short, he found almost nothing in over half a century in the New World that was not ordered better at home. Little wonder, then, that he saw much good in the Tory cause when, a few years after he arrived in America, revolution tore apart his churchpeople, nor that he finally turned over the remnants of his Swedish congregations at Swedesboro and Penn's Neck to the (recently Tory) Anglicans shortly after the war. He spent his declining days in Philadelphia, with all of the virtues and vices of a confirmed conservative, friend and compeer of all the great men of his day.

The remnants of the early Swedish settlements in New Jersey are all too few; the beautiful Old Swede's Church at Swedesboro; Swedish and Finnish names on gravestones in the cemeteries there and at St. George's Church (Churchtown) and Friesburg; a Swedish log building still standing as a part of an old house; the sleepy town of Repaupo still carrying the reputation of being New Jersey's most Swedish community; some traditions of Swedish beginnings in the settlement at Port Elizabeth on the Maurice River; the Swedish (and Finnish) names of Mullica and Steelman remembered in New Jersey towns and rivers; the stones of Fort Elfsborg now beneath the Delaware; a few Swedish family names still borne proudly by the people of Gloucester and Salem counties. Overwhelmed by numbers of English, German, and Scotch Irish neighbors, it would be hard to trace to the Swedes of New Jersey any distinct contribution to the ways of America. It would be hard, too, to find a trace of any branch of the Delaware in the main stream, yet no thoughtful person will doubt that it is there.

IX

THE JERSEY DUTCH

THE DUTCH BEGINNINGS of New Netherland had a peculiar vitality. The people, before and after the Dutch occupation, were by no means all Dutch. There were settlements, such as the Hackensack French Patent, in New Jersey, and New Paltz and Harlem, in New York, where most of the people were French. At New Brunswick large numbers of Englishmen settled themselves among the Dutch. Before long they were all talking Dutch; indeed many of them, if asked, would probably have said that they were Jersey Dutch, though their names might have been Jean Demarest or Richard Berry, and the accent of the one might have come from Amiens and the other from the Island of Barbados. All of them attended the Dutch Reformed Church, which was not remarkable, since there were no other churches in the Dutch country for a long time. They all soon began to build their houses in Jersey Dutch style, to eat Jersey Dutch food, and to give their children Jersey Dutch names, in short to adopt the whole Jersey Dutch way of life.

The persistence of Dutch habits, manners, and customs had nothing whatever to do with Dutch nationalism; it traced to little more than a cheerful self-confidence that the ways of the Dutch were better ways. Indeed, it is hard not to agree that there was something special about the few hundred Dutch men and women who lived in New

Netherland when the British seized it, and put their stamp so strongly on the future of America.

What impressed most observers was Dutch industry, frugality, and assiduous perseverance in the means of striving, as an English officer put it during the Revolutionary War. They were ambitious, another wrote at about the same time, to appear always neat and cleanly, and never to complain of an empty purse.

When Washington Irving wrote about the home of the "thriving, contented, liberal-hearted" Dutch farmer, Baltus Van Tassel, who "seldom . . . set either his eyes or his thoughts beyond the boundaries of his own farm . . . satisfied with his own wealth, but not proud of it," he was describing a Dutch farm whose like he had seen a hundred times:

. . . one of those spacious farmhouses, with . . . low projecting eaves forming a piazza along the front. . . . Under this, were hung flails, harness, various utensils of husbandry, and nets for fishing in the neighboring river. Benches were built along the sides for summer use; and a great spinning wheel at one end and a churn at the other showed the purposes to which this important porch might be devoted. . . .

And again, when he wrote of Van Tassel's vast barn, with every crevice bursting with the treasures of the farm, the flail busily resounding within it from morning to night, the fat cattle, and the barnyard full of cackling fowl, he was describing the general air of hearty abundance that characterized Dutch farms throughout all of New York and New Jersey. The Abram Hoagland place at Six-Mile Run, for example,

. . . was perhaps as near perfection as any in those times. . . . The out-buildings were large, well constructed, and as numerous as comfort and convenience could possibly demand. In addition to the dwelling, there was a spring house, used exclusively as a dairy in summer, with plastered stone walls and ceiling and a flagstone floor, having a stream of pure cold spring water flowing through it. . . . There was a large cider house, with mill and press, for home use and for the convenience of the neighbors. There were shops with their work benches, in which, in the winter, when time would permit, they would be employed in making many things necessary in working the farm, saving the expenses attending the employment of mechanics. The harness for plowing and common work was made of flax or tow, pulled out and spun in the winter evenings by the boys. . . . The girls performed their part by plying the flax and woolen wheels, and by their industrious and economical efforts materials were prepared and woven by which the family were clothed at all seasons. . . . The family had its tan vat and tanned its own leather. Having manufactured the materials, the tailor and shoemaker would come to the house and there make them up into garments, etc. . . . The farm was well supplied with fruit. There were all the then known kinds of cherries, some of which are now unknown, thirteen different kinds of pears, also apricots, English strawberries, and all the choicer kinds of apples.*

The overflowing abundance of their farms did nothing to change Dutch frugality. A French officer who visited Pompton during the Revolution was amazed to see Dutchmen content, as he put it, to be only spectators of their own wealth, living modestly in the midst of farms that rich men would have been proud to own anywhere else in the world. "Their houses . . . ," he said, "[are] very simple and small, only the barns lofty and spacious." What he did not see was that Dutch self-denial, as much as hard work, was responsible for their wealth. Too proud to complain of an empty purse, they were not too proud to do the things that kept their purses full. Peter Kalm, the Swedish botanist and theologian, who traveled widely through the colonies in the 1750's found the same thing. Dutchmen, he said, were

. . . more thrifty in their homes than the English. . . . They are more frugal in preparing food, and seldom is more of it

* Ralph Voorhees, "Franklin Township Historical Notes," *Somerset County Historical Quarterly* (Rutgers University Library).

seen on the table than is consumed, and sometimes hardly that. They are careful not to load up the table with food as the English are accustomed to do. They are not so given to drink as the latter, and the punch bowl does not make a daily round in their households . . .

Many a Dutchman ate the same unchanging meal of *sappaan* for supper every day from the cradle to the grave. *Sappaan* (pronounced "spawn") was the Indian name for a porridge made of corn meal. "Served in a good sized dish," Kalm said, "a large hole is made in its center, into which milk is poured, and then one proceeds to help himself."

Frugal as they were, Dutchmen's other meals were by no means as plain as their suppers of corn meal mush and milk. As winter came on, the good *huis vrouw* would bake thirty or forty mince pies at one time, and put aside a stock of *rolletjes* (chopped beef and suet, seasoned and spiced, rolled, sewed up in tripe, then boiled for a day or more and served sliced, either cold or fried), sausages, cookies and crullers, *beuling* (buckwheat with *stroop* [molasses] and spices, made into a stiff pudding and served cold or fried), pumpkin bread and pumpkin *koondjes* (boiled pumpkin mixed with Indian meal and

Southern View of Somerville, c. 1840. One Reformed Church is the second spire from the right, the other is on the extreme left.

fried in small cakes). Peter Kalm's Dutch landlady at Albany, Mrs. Vischer, introduced him to *kool slaa*. She took the inner leaves of a head of cabbage, he said, and cut them into long strips, put them on a platter, poured oil and vinegar upon them and added salt and pepper while mixing the shredded cabbage. "This dish has a very pleasing flavor and tastes better than one can imagine," Kalm said. Mrs. Vischer assured him that many of her guests had asked for her recipe and had made it themselves when they returned to their homes.

The Dutch were proud of their plain Dutch ways and looked on the neighboring colonies as lacking their homely virtues. Their neighbors, of course, for their part, were sometimes less impressed, feeling that some of the plain Dutch ways verged on boorishness. Kalm, though his views were colored by an inclination to judge people by the deference they showed him, leaves no doubt on this score. He observed that even in New York City, the Dutch, both in speech and outward manners, were not as polite and well-bred as the English, and still less so than the French, though he conceded that their intentions were good and that they showed their kindly spirit in all they did. Perhaps forgetting that the Frenchmen he had met in Canada were high officials, and that his acquaintance among English farmers and workmen was small, the Dutch seemed to him to suffer by comparison. A Frenchman, he said, would always say *"donnez à monsieur,"* and an Englishman "give the gentleman," but the Dutch never said anything other than *"giw dese man,"* and women were treated with no more formality. The difference between the English and the Dutch, Kalm felt, was like that between a refined merchant in the city and a rather crude farmer in the country, adding however, that it was well to remember that there are exceptions to every rule. Evidently having suffered from the practice, he observed that

if several persons of Dutch extraction should come into a house . . . as many as could be accommodated would sit down about the fire. Then if any others should happen in, they pretended not to see them. Even though they saw them and conversed with them, they did not consider it wise to move from the fire and give the others a little room, but they sat there like lifeless statues. The French and English always made room by moving a little.*

At another time, in a better mood, he said that Dutchmen in and around New York were civil, obliging, just in prices, and sincere, and, though they were not ceremonious, yet they were well meaning and honest, and their promises could be relied on. He made it plain, however, that this did not include the Dutchmen at Albany, New York. The streets of the towns were often very dirty, with cattle roaming there in summer, but the Dutch houses were spotless. "The women," Kalm wrote, "rise early, go to sleep late and are almost superstitiously clean in regard to the floors, which are frequently scoured several times in the week." In the towns, in the summer, when the work was done, the family gathered on the front stoop, spending an hour or two in chatting, with the good lady of the house, as often as not, leaning over the lower half of the front door and joining in the talk.

The huge Dutch kitchen was the family sitting room, the parlor being reserved for weddings and funerals. The kitchen fireplace, big enough to roast an ox, with its great brick oven on one side, occupied nearly the entire wall on one side of the room. A spider, a flat iron pan, sat over the dying coals at one side, and from the trammels and pot hooks of a long iron crane hung iron pots, griddles, and kettles, one of which was always kept filled with hot water. The trunk of a good-sized hickory tree served as a backlog, and a rich base of hickory coals glowed in front.

Many a young Dutchman sat before a huge fire in the kitchen of his Bergen County home on winter nights

* Adolph B. Benson (ed.), *Peter Kalm's Travels in North America* (New York, 1937), II, 628.

Interior Dirck Dey Mansion, Preakness
Courtesy of Mr. Richard A. Dey

while the *storm king* shrieked down the chimney and
piled snow against the windows, and his *grootvader* told
of the *spooks* and witches and Indians of long ago: about
the witch who lived in Preakness, in the gap of the
mountains, where no one could drive cattle or sheep
past her house unless she stood in the doorway and
greeted the drover; or about the time he had been forced
to stop his wagon on the King's Highway and put a sign
made of twigs, something like a figure 4, in the road to
keep witches from following him; or about the ghosts of
the American soldiers, still looking for the Tories who
gave them poisoned milk near the *spook* bridge in
Sluckup, or about the *spook* that troubled Sele Van
Giesen of Totowa until he put a silver musket ball in

his gun and shot it. Young Dutchmen did not have to be told, when they saw an older sister swinging a whip around the churn eight times in her left hand, that she was frustrating a witch who had been trying to keep her from fetching butter.

The garrets over the one-story houses were as fascinating as the kitchens. Piles of apples and nuts occupied the corners, and from the rafters were festooned strings of red peppers, clusters of seed corn, and bunches of dried herbs, filling the air with their spicy aroma, while tables bearing dozens of mince and pumpkin pies were overhung with strings of sausage.

Jersey Dutch families had a great fondness for particular names: David among Ackermans and Demarests, Johannes among Blauvelts and Harings, Abraham among Mabies, Paulus among Martensens, Adrian among Posts, Wiert and Seba among Bantas, Laurence among Van Buskirks, Guiliam among Bertholfs, Reynier among Van Giesens. At one time, a stranger in Bergen would have had to try to distinguish among Van Hornes named John, John's John, Trinches' John, Mill Creek John, Canal Bridge John, and probably others. A young man of Schraalenburgh with a prominent nose, baptized Abraham Demarest, was called *"Hookie Brom"* all his life.

It is hard not to think that Jersey Dutchmen enjoyed their reputation for these small eccentricities; that Dutchmen who sat in front of the fire for hours, tranquilly smoking their pipes, and lost in contemplation of the Biblical scenes on the blue and white tiles with which the fireplace was decorated, knew that their solemn deliberations were not unobserved. "Stoffel" Van Riper, the bumbling leader of an early militia company in the Passaic Valley, was probably not displeased to know that all of the children in the neighborhood chanted

> Stoffel Van Riper! Stoffel Van Riper!
> Turn out your toes when you go round a corner,

or unaware that when he backed down his own cellar

steps at the head of his militia company, people would talk about it for years. (He shouted at his poor wife, when she ran down the stairs to help him: "Go away, woman! What do you know about war?") Local people claimed that he once had to call on Captain Garrabrant to keep his doughty warriors from parading across a newly planted field, which Garrabrant did by shouting "Halt!" Stoffel, they said, shook his head and asked "Why couldn't I think of that?" It may have been another case of nature copying art. Washington Irving's works were as well known in the Jersey Dutch country as they were elsewhere.

Though Jersey Dutch children were instructed in both the English and Dutch languages from the earliest days of New Jersey, "in their houses and among themselves,"

Communipaw, c. 1870
Winfield, "History of Hudson County"

Peter Kalm reported, Dutchmen "always spoke Dutch, so that rarely is an English word heard." The practice continued long after they had become perfectly at ease in English and dressed and acted exactly like their English neighbors.

Jersey Dutch was spoken in back-country places as late as 1900, two hundred years after the last Jersey Dutchman came to America. Two somewhat supercilious New Yorkers on a jaunt through New Jersey in 1871 found that the descendants of the early Dutch settlers in the neighborhood of Franklin Lake spoke "a hideous jargon called Jersey Dutch, a melange of English and Low Dutch," and in 1873, a Holland Dutchman was astonished to be welcomed in a remote village with the mixed English-Dutch greeting: *"Main Heer, ik kan speek Duitch."* The Dutch language seemed to Jersey Dutchmen to have a ring of sincerity that English lacked. It was, they felt, peculiarly suited to sermons. When an English clergyman said to John Henry Goetschius, referring to his solemn and severe manner in the pulpit: "It always seems to me, when I hear you preach, that the law must have been given in the Dutch language." "Very likely," said Mr. Goetschius, who came from Zurich, Switzerland, "and I have always thought that English must have been the language in which the serpent spoke to Eve in Paradise."

Dutch preaching continued long after Dutch congregations were fluent in English. Though they themselves soon began keeping their own records in English, the Consistory of Hackensack and Schraalenburgh in 1791 allowed Domine Solomon Froeligh to preach in English only on alternate Sunday afternoons. Even in New York, English was not used in the Dutch Reformed Church until 1764. New Brunswick, partly English in background, did not hear English sermons before 1773, and it was 1793 before Dutch was discontinued there. In 1811 preaching in English was begun at Paramus, but Dutch seems to have been used in afternoon services there and elsewhere well down into the 1860's and 1870's.

The English preaching in Dutch churches may have left something to be desired. An English officer attended Dutch church services during the war, at which the local domine was trying out his English on the congregation. The officer, it is said, told his friends that he was astonished at the similarity of Dutch and English; that he had been able to understand a good deal of the sermon; and that if he had realized his talents as a linguist he would have learned Dutch years before. Domine Schoonmaker once attempted to conclude a marriage service in English with the statement "I now pronounce

Tunis R. Cooper Chair Factory, Schraalenburgh, c. 1880
Courtesy Mr. and Mrs. William H. Pratt

you man and wife and one flesh." What he said was: "I pronounce you one beef."

The celebrated Cooper chair factory in Schraalenburgh, which burned in the 1890's, carried on its business with its workmen in Jersey Dutch to the end, notwithstanding that most of the ancestors of Schraalenburgh Dutchmen came from the nearby French Patent, and many bore French, Scottish, or English names. "Tappan is still very Dutch," a visitor wrote in 1899. "Hundreds who speak the tongue still live within a five-mile radius of the church." In Bergen, in the shadow of New York City,

. . . the Dutch language prevailed almost exclusively to within the last half century [i.e., to 1850], especially in the intercourse of the inhabitants with each other; and even after church services were regularly held in English, the occasional afternoon preaching in Dutch was hailed with great satisfaction and rejoicing by the older people of the congregation.

In some cases "Jersey" or "Bergen County" Dutch was still the vernacular of the descendants of the original Netherland settlers in the early years of the twentieth century, a student of local dialects has said. "Up to [1880] this was the common idiom of many rural districts in northern New Jersey, employed alike by Dutch, English, German and Dutch settlers. . . . It now [1919] survives only in the memories of some two hundred old persons, nearly all of them over seventy years of age."

It is said that every man becomes a hero to his biographer. It would be hard to study the Jersey Dutch without coming to admire them. They bore many of the traits that we have come to consider pridefully as American. Some of these may have been brought from Holland or France; some suggest the transforming power of the New World. They had a deep self-assurance that spared them almost completely from the twin sins of envy and fear. If some lack of imagination went with their self-assurance, that was a small enough price to pay for their virtues. They were happy to assume (if they considered the matter at all) that others admired their plain Dutch ways as much as they did. They ignored the arts they thought effete but excelled at those they thought practical. They were far wiser than they were clever, though of course they were not always wise. They were tolerant to a fault of the ways of others but slow to accept them. Faithful to the Biblical injunction to be diligent in business and instant in prayer, they felt no compulsion whatever to change other people who were not.

They were fortunate to have been Dutchmen during the brief golden age of the Netherlands. They were equally fortunate to have been Britons in the golden age of British America, and Americans in the early days of the American frontier. But most of all, America is fortunate that these proud, cheerful, tolerant, virtuous, and successful people laid part of her foundations.

BIBLIOGRAPHICAL NOTE

THE HISTORY of the earliest Dutch settlements in New Jersey is, of course, a part of the history of New Netherland as a whole. The fundamental source materials for any study of New Netherland have been used and re-used in many histories. The principal documents were brought back to the State of New York from Holland in 1841 by John Romeyn Brodhead, a descendant of a Jersey Dutch pastor, and these and some subsequently discovered records were translated and published by the State of New York between 1856 and 1883 as the monumental *Documents Relative to the Colonial History of the State of New York,* edited by E. B. O'Callaghan. These "Colonial Documents" are the source for most of the early histories of New York and New Jersey. O'Callaghan's *Calendar of Historical Manuscripts in the Office of the Secretary of State* (Albany, New York, 1856) is a summary of other valuable documents about the early days of New Netherland, which were unfortunately burned in a fire in the New York State House in 1911. The archives of the City of Amsterdam have other material in the form of notarial records which include American data. *The Records of New Amsterdam from 1653 to 1674* (New York, 1897), edited by Berthold Fernow, is a record of the New Amsterdam city government and its judicial cases during those 21 years. The handsomely illustrated six-volume *Iconography of Manhattan Island* (New York, 1915-1928), by I. N. Phelps Stokes, is a collection of substantially everything that a wealthy and talented collector could bring together on the subject of New Amsterdam and New York. E. T. Corwin's seven-volume *Ecclesiastical Records of the State of New York* (Albany, 1905) contains all of the records of the church authorities in Amsterdam relating to the early Dutch churches in New York and New Jersey. *Narratives of New Netherland* (New York, 1909), edited by J. Franklin Jameson, is a selection of some of the best material from the Colonial Documents and from certain other Dutch sources, some of which is not available elsewhere. *The Journal of Jasper Danckaerts* (New York, 1913), published as one of the same series of "Original Narratives of Early American History," is also useful. The third volume of Charles M. Andrew's *The Colonial Period of American History* (New Haven, 1937), is a scholarly study of the Dutch and other efforts at colonization in America. J. R. Brodhead, *History of New Netherland* (New York, 1858), though very old, is considered by many to be the best detailed early history of New Netherland. It includes much material from the now lost Albany records. E. B. O'Callaghan, *History of New Netherland* (New York, 1848), is another similar history. In 1959, the archivist of the City of Amsterdam, Dr. Simon Hart, published a scholarly study of the earliest fur traders in the Hudson River valley as the *Prehistory of New Netherland Company* (Amsterdam, 1959), which used original Dutch source material and cast much new light on the beginnings of Dutch relations with America.

In the scholarly *Province of East New Jersey 1609-1702* (Princeton, 1962), Dr. John E. Pomfret placed the disorganized material about the Dutch beginnings of New Jersey into orderly and understandable form, and his *Province of West New Jersey 1609-1702* (Princeton, 1956) does much the same task for the Dutch settlements on the Delaware. The Holland Society Year Book for the year 1917 includes a carefully written *Story of New Amsterdam,* by Professor William R. Shephard. Henry H. Kessler and Eugene Rachlis have recently written a most readable and authentic account of New Amsterdam in the mid-seventeenth century entitled *Peter Stuyvesant and His New York* (New York, 1959).

Turning more specifically to New Jersey, almost a hundred years ago C. H. Winfield, a lawyer of Jersey City, wrote an amazingly detailed *History of the County of Hudson, New Jersey* (New York, 1874) in which he brought together almost everything that could possibly be collected about the settlers of that part of the State of New Jersey, using the Colonial Documents, the Albany Records, and the Amsterdam Court Records extensively, along with his own great talent for genealogical research. It is a valuable source book on the early Dutch in New Jersey. In 1846, The New Jersey Historical Society published *East Jersey under the Proprietary Governments, etc.,* by William A. Whitehead. It includes some material about the relations of Dutchmen to the early English rulers, but is oriented toward the English settlers. Dingman Versteeg, the translator of most of the Dutch Church Records for the Holland Society, published a paper entitled *"The Founding of Jersey City . . ."* in the Holland Society Year Book for 1914, which includes many colorful details about the early days of Bergen, as does a little volume by Daniel Van Winkle entitled *Old Bergen, History and Reminiscences* (Jersey City, 1902) and another published by the Trust Company of New Jersey in 1921, entitled *History of Hudson County and of the Old Village of Bergen* (Jersey City, 1921). There are many fine small histories of Dutch Reformed churches in New Jersey and several fine genealogies of Dutch families. Among the church histories are E. T. Corwin, *A History of the Classis of Paramus* (New York, 1902), E. T. Corwin, *Manual of the Reformed Church in America* (4th ed.; New York, 1902), Abraham Messler, *Memorial Sermons, Forty Years at Raritan . . .* (New York, 1873), B. C. Taylor, *Annals of the Classis of Bergen, etc.* (New York, 1857), *Tercentenary Studies, 1928, Reformed Church in America* (New York, 1928), T. B. Romeyn, *Historical Discourse on . . . the First Reformed (Dutch) Church in Hackensack, N. J.* (New York, 1870), Cornelius T. Demarest, *A Lamentation Over the Rev. Solomon Froeligh* (New York, 1827),

E. T. Corwin, *Historical Discourse on . . . the Reformed Dutch Church at Millstone* (New York, 1866), Richard H. Steele, *Historical Discourse . . . the Reformed Dutch Church, New Brunswick, N. J.* (New Brunswick, 1867), Henry P. Thompson, *History of the Reformed Church at Readington, N. J.* (New York, 1882), and G. W. Labaw, *Preakness and the Preakness Reformed Church* (New York, 1902). Among the many genealogical sources are T. N. Banta, *The Banta Genealogy* (New York, 1893), L. L. Blauvelt, *The Blauvelt Family Genealogy* (East Orange, 1957), *Family of Joris Dirckson Brinckerhoff* (New York, 1887), Walter Christie, *Genealogy of the Christie Family* (Bergenfield, 1919), David Cole, *Cole Genealogy* (Yonkers, New York, 1864), W. H. S. Demarest, *The Demarest Family* (New Brunswick, 1938), George O. Zabriskie, *The Zabriskie Family* (Salt Lake City, Utah, 1963), T. L. Van Norden, *The Van Norden Family* (Lancaster, Pa., 1923); W. T. Westervelt, *Genealogy of the Westervelt Family* (New York, 1905). Rosalie F. Bailey, *Pre-Revolutionary Dutch Houses and Families* (New York, 1936) is a large volume with many beautiful photographs of Dutch colonial houses, some of which have since been destroyed, and genealogical material about their builders. W. J. Lane, *From Indian Trail to Iron Horse* (Princeton, 1939) is a scholarly study of the early roads and transportation in New Jersey and Nelson R. Burr, *Education in New Jersey* (Princeton, 1942), one of the same series on New Jersey history published by Princeton University Press, though it ignores the important academy founded by New Jersey Dutchmen at Hackensack under Peter Wilson, is otherwise most thorough in its study of Jersey Dutch education. The recently published *Early Maps of North America,* by Robert M. Lunny, fortunately tends to include maps of interest to Jerseymen, including the celebrated Vingboons *Map of New Netherland* of 1639. The original Vingboons maps are in the Library of Congress, along with a large number of other early maps of New Jersey. The New York Public Library and the New York Historical Society

Library have other early maps of New Jersey; and the papers of Sir Henry Clinton, in the Clements Library of the University of Michigan, contain many maps of New Jersey at the time of the American Revolution. In the case of Hudson County, Dr. D. Stanton Hammond has prepared a map showing landholdings at and after the Dutch surrender (*Bergen Town and Township . . . Manuscript map . . .* compiled by D. Stanton Hammond, J. D. [Bound Brook, 1943]). The Rutgers University Library has many manuscripts and rare books on early New Jersey history, one of many of them being a complete set of the *Somerset County Historical Quarterly* which gives many details about Dutch life in middle Jersey. Another great historian of the Jersey Dutch was William Nelson, who is said to have almost given up his law practice in Paterson to pursue his hobby of collecting documents and data about New Jersey—to the point where some of his contemporaries shunned him as "Snoopy" Nelson. He helped to edit the *History of Bergen and Passaic Counties, New Jersey* (Philadelphia, 1882) which sets that volume apart from the many similar books of the day. He also wrote the monumental *History of Paterson* (Paterson, 1920) with much Dutch material. Other county histories published at the same time and many local histories are useful.

The *Archives of the State of New Jersey, First and Second Series* (Paterson, 1880, etc.) were also edited in part by William Nelson and are a primary source for study of New Jersey history. John W. Barber and Henry Howe, *Historical Collections of the State of New Jersey* (Newark, 1844), the *Proceedings of The New Jersey Historical Society* and *The New York Historical Society Collections* are also valuable. James Riker, *Harlem, Its Origin and Early Annals* (New York, 1881), discusses at length the Huguenot families who moved to New Jersey.

Extensive use has been made of the Journal of Peter Kalm, the Swedish botanist who traveled in America in the 1740's and 1750's: Adolph B. Benson (ed.), *Peter Kalm's Travels in North America* (New York, 1937).

H. M. Muhlenberg, *The Journals of Henry Melchior Muhlenberg* (Philadelphia, 1942), shows a perceptive German clergyman's view of some of the Dutch. T. J. Wertenbaker, *The Founding of America: The Middle Colonies* (New York, 1938) is the best study of the confrontation of Dutch and English ways in New York and New Jersey, and includes much detailed material on the early Dutch settlers. Emily J. DeForest, *A Walloon Family in America* (New York, 1911) includes useful material about early Dutch and Walloon life in New Amsterdam. C. A. Weslager, *Dutch Explorers, Traders and Settlers in the Delaware Valley (1609-1674)* (Philadelphia, 1961) describes the early Dutch explorations and settlements on the Delaware.

Separate source material covers the settlements on the Minisink. Barber and Howe and Samuel W. Eager, *An Outline History of Orange County* (Newburgh, 1846-1847) have early publications of the story of the mine holes told by the Pennsylvania surveyors. Marius Schoonmaker's *History of Kingston* (New York, 1888) has some material on the families who later moved to Minisink. The old Dutch *Records of the Mackrackemech and Menissinck Churches* (Port Lewis, 1899) and L. W. Brodhead, *The Delaware Water Gap* (Philadelphia, 1870) also have other genealogical data on these families. Charles E. Stickney, *A History of the Minisink Region* (Middletown, N. Y., 1867) and *The First Sussex Centenary* (Newark, 1854) are good histories of the region. C. G. Hine, *The Old Mine Road* (New Brunswick, 1963 [reprint]) and Amelia S. Decker, *That Ancient Trail* (Trenton, 1942) are useful informal books on the subject.

Almost anything that is written about the Swedish and Finnish settlements on the Delaware is perforce a summary of the monumental work of Dr. Amandus Johnson, *The Swedish Settlements on the Delaware,* a two-volume study published in Lancaster, Pennsylvania, in 1911. Dr. Johnson, who is still actively pursuing his interest in the early Swedish settlements in America 52 years later, modestly says that he would have written some of his material differently if he were writing today, but it is hard to see that anything in this great work could be written differently or that any material amount of new information could be added. In many ways the Swedish settlements support a more extensive scholarly literature than the larger and more important Dutch settlements. The learned Swedish clergymen who came to America wrote extensively about America, and the Dutch clergymen, though equally learned, did not, perhaps because the Swedish clergymen took a more detached view of America than their Dutch counterparts, who were often too actively involved in their congregation's activities to comment broadly upon them. *Swedish Commentators on America 1638-1865* by Esther E. Larson (New York, 1963) is a comprehensive guide to manuscript and printed material on the Swedes. W. M. Reynolds (ed.), *A History of New Sweden . . . by Israel Acrelius* (Phila., 1874) and Amandus Johnson (ed.), *Journal and Biography of Nicholas Collin 1746-1831* (Phila., 1936) preserve detailed and scholarly accounts of America. A recent biography of Carl Magnus Wrangel, published in Sweden, adds much about the revivals among the Swedes. Nils Jacobson, *Bland Svenskamerikaner och Gustavianer* (Stockholm, 1953), and H. M. Muhlenberg's *Journal* touches on the same subject.

Peter Kalm, mentioned above, primarily a botanist but for a time Swedish Lutheran minister at Swedesboro, wrote one of the most informative early books about America. Adolph B. Benson, ed. *Peter Kalm's Travels in North America* (New York, 1937). Peter Lindestrom, an engineer with Governor Rising, wrote an account of his experiences in America, Amandus Johnson (ed.), *Geographica Americae, by Peter Lindestrom* (Phila., 1925). Governor Printz' correspondence is also useful. See Amandus Johnson (ed.), *Instructions for Johan Printz* (Phila., 1930). The church records at Raccoon (Swedesboro) and Penns Neck include many candid observations about the church people. See *The Records of the Swedish Lutheran Churches at Raccoon and Penns Neck* (Elizabeth, 1938). See also *Records of Holy Trinity* (Old Swedes) Church (Wilmington, 1890).

Benjamin Ferris wrote an early history of Wilmington, Delaware, with some material relating to New Jersey, *A History of the Original Settlements on the Delaware . . .* (Wilmington, 1846) and Rev. Jehu C. Clay wrote an early history of the Swedes on the Delaware, *Annals of the Swedes on the Delaware* (Phila., 1858) now of course, superseded by Johnson's monumental work, and E. A. Louhi and J. H. Wuorinen have written the story from a Finnish viewpoint, Louhi being sharply critical of the Swede's disposition to ignore the Finns' part in the history of the settlement: E. A. Louhi, *The Delaware Finns* (New York, 1925); J. H. Wuorinen, *The Finns on The Delaware* (New York, 1938). The late Christopher Ward, lawyer and historian, of Wilmington, Delaware, wrote a short book, *New Sweden on the Delaware* (Philadelphia, 1938), in connection with the tercentenary observances of the Swedish landing in America. One of the most readable books on the subject is *The Swedes and Finns in New Jersey* (Elizabeth, 1938), a book of the Federal Writers' Project, published in 1938 as part of the American Guide Series. Either through modesty or through bureaucratic regulations, the author of this splendid book is not identified, but the Raccoon and Penns Neck Church Records, also published by the Federal Writers' Project, suggests that her name was Irene Fuhlbruegge. The photographers who were responsible for the beautiful illustrations cannot be identified. *Narratives of Pennsylvania, West Jersey, and Delaware* (A. C. Myers, ed. New York, 1912) and *The History of the Counties of Gloucester, Cumberland, and Salem, New Jersey* (Philadelphia, 1883) have some useful details about the Swedish settlements in New Jersey. Some of the other source materials are Justin Winsor, *Narrative and Critical History of America*, IV (Boston, 1884), C. A. Weslager, *Dutch Explorers, Traders and Settlers in the Delaware Valley 1609-1664* (Philadelphia, 1961), mentioned above, and Gregory B. Keen, *The Descendants of Jöran Kyn of New Sweden* (Philadelphia, 1913).

INDEX